IS YOUR "NET" WORKING?

A COMPLETE GUIDE TO BUILDING CONTACTS AND CAREER VISIBILITY

Anne Boe
Bettie B. Youngs, Ph.D.

WILEY

John Wiley & Sons, Inc.

New York • Chichester • Brisbane • Toronto • Singapore

Publisher: Stephen Kippur
Editor: Katherine Schowalter
Managing Editor: Frank Grazioli
Editing, Design, and Production: Tage Publishing Service

Library of Congress Cataloging-in-Publication Data

Boe, Anne, 1946–
  Is your "net" working? : a complete guide to building contacts and career visibility / Anne Boe, Bettie B. Youngs.
    p.   cm.
  Bibliography: p.
  ISBN 0-471-61547-1
  1. Success in business. 2. Social networks.   I. Youngs, Bettie
B.   II. Title.   III. Title: Is your networking?
HF5386.B59 1989
650.1—dc19   88-28086
                                                                CIP

Printed in the United States of America
89 90 10 9 8 7 6 5 4 3

ACKNOWLEDGMENTS

Over the past twenty years, we have worked with literally thousands of people in over 40 countries. Though we did the teaching, we listened and learned. As we shared with others, they shared with us. For those cherished exchanges, we thank the many individuals who contributed to this book. Interdependence is essential in researching and writing a book. Our illusion of independence was quickly tossed aside and replaced with a reality of community. For their help and support on this project special thanks to our National Speaking Association (NSA) friends and colleagues, Lee Shapiro, Cavett Robert, Lee Robert, Joe Jeff Goldblatt, Jeff Lange, Dr. Charles Geeslin, Dave Nightingale, Bobbie Gee, Tom Hinton, Dick Maches, Brian Tracy, Jack Canfield and Mark Victor Hansen.

We have been inspired and encouraged by the support of the many wonderful friends and colleagues who so generously gave of their time and expertise. To Mary Louise Martin, Helen Bloomfield, Sharon Wilson, Barbara and Sherman Hickman, Cheri Hart, Tony Alessandra, Gerald Conley, and Vic Preisser, who not only have helped each of us build our careers over the years, but continue to support us in our personal and professional growth, a loving thank you. Without the able and generously caring help of Catherine Baldwin, this book would not have moved beyond the manuscript stage. And to our special and valued clients, Gary Robertson, Steve Bailey, Ron Fellows, Judy McCartney, and John Logan, a deep sense of appreciation. For their invaluable advice and counsel, special recognition goes to management consultant, author, and long time friend Joe D. Batten, and to Wendy Rue, Founder and Past President of the National Association of Female Executives. Wendy's friendship in particular began many years ago as she trusted our decision to sponsor a major conference in Canada and begin what was to become one of the largest professional networks in the world (NAFE).

And of course, appreciations are never complete without special praise to our parents and families, not only for their love, support, patience and understanding in the task of writing a book, but for the ways they have influenced and shaped our lives. For that, we thank our parents, Everett and Arlene Burres and Milton and Lenore Weis.

CONTENTS

To our friends and business associates

INTRODUCTION

Suppose you could reduce your workload and increase your productivity—that you could combine elements of social fun with business obligations. The formula for such an enticing endeavor is networking. NETWORKING is a skill. Networking is a vital, vibrant, growing area of business that more of us are incorporating into our outlines for success. Networking enhances the quality of your work and enriches the relationships that are a part of our work place. This book is a blueprint for mastering that skill in a relatively short time using determination and persistence.

This book was written to share with you some of the networking skills and techniques we have developed and tested over the years. Along with specific suggestions and exercises, we present real life case studies showing how networking is a significant part of being efficient and effective in our roles. While we recommend that you read chapter one first to get an overview of networking, after that feel free to skip around. Each individual has his or her own particular reasons for wanting to learn more about networking; one chapter might be of more interest to you than the others. Each chapter covers one specific area or element of networking, gives suggestions geared towards using networking to meet your goals in that area, and presents exercises to help you improve your networking skills. Real life scenarios vividly illustrate the major points, outlining for you the dynamics of networking. You will probably come back to this book again and again as networking takes an ever increasing role in your life. Networking is a skill that can be practiced and improved constantly. Our goal in this book is to help you do just that.

First, we give you an overview of networking, what it is, how it can affect you, and predictions of how important networking will be in the future. Next, we explore the concept of power, and how networking can help you get the information that gives you that power. And don't forget, you are also part of the networks of others. To network effectively, you give, as well as receive, and we share with you the best ways to communicate your knowledge to others. We help you develop a networking plan to keep track of the favors you grant and the information you give, and how to follow up and get the maximum benefit from your networking skills. We all know that job referrals are a major benefit of networking. The intricasies of getting and giving referrals are covered in detail in Chapter 6. We offer realistic suggestions that can help you understand how to use networking to meet both your professional and your personal goals, and to help you visualize where you want to be in the future. If you work out of your home, you may be wondering whether a networking book is relevant to you. We recognize the growing number of homeworkers, and offer a chapter dealing with your special needs. Whether you work out of your home or in an office, please don't skip this chapter. You probably know people who are homeworkers, and can better use the information in this chapter to network with other homeworkers. Everyone is involved in sales or customer service in one way or another. We constantly sell ourselves and our qualifications, our companies and our services, our knowledge and our skills. The final chapter of this book covers how to network in sales and customer service, including a six-point plan for creating an ongoing network with customers or clients.

1
NETWORKING IN THE '90s AND BEYOND

*L*ynne is a faculty member of a large university teaching management science. She is nearing tenure, but having second thoughts about remaining at her job. She has the standard "Could the grass be greener elsewhere?" worries. Although she makes good money and has the respect of the professional community, she feels that there is little future for her; she could be teaching the same courses year in and year out for the next two decades. In brief, Lynne is trying to decide whether to remain at the university, or open her own consulting business. She needs to know whether there will be business out there for her, whether she can make a living and have a future doing on a private basis what she does for the university.

Lynne sits down at her computer, and begins making lists of her contacts. She soon finds that she knows people in many different businesses, large and small. Her years of teaching evening graduate courses (which attract primarily working adults) let her meet and gain the respect of dozens of people who work at the firms with which she wants to consult. Lynne makes calls, follows them up with letters, and soon meets with the people her former students suggest. Those students are instrumental in telling their bosses and employment personnel about Lynne's skills and what she can offer to their business. After several meetings, Lynne has enough interest (and two signed contracts!) to convince her that there is a demand for her services in the private sector. Slowly but steadily she builds up a client base, getting more and more referrals, handling more and more jobs. At first, she continues to work for the university, doing her consulting in the evenings and weekends. When she is confident that her name is well enough known in the community to ensure her continuing to get work, she quits her position at the university. The decision is not made lightly, but turns out to be the right one. Today, Lynne is a successful management consultant, doing work with firms across the nation, and with their branches overseas. She performs a variety of tasks, enjoys meeting new people, loves traveling, and is making a good living doing exactly what she wants to do. Her knowledge and talent get her the jobs, but her networking skills get her the interviews.

Hal is an attorney. He has been working for a firm for several years, and is eager to be made a partner. The senior partners have told him that in order to become a partner, he will have to bring more business into the office. Since Hal has strong feelings against advertising, he has no idea where to begin. He calls several friends of his for suggestions. They suggest he strengthen and then use his networking skills.

Hal decides to take their advice. He assesses his strengths: a friendly personality and a large group of friends. He asks several of his friends to take him to meetings with them, going to VFW, charity, and Rotary get-togethers. He joins a breakfast club of working men and women who meet once a week. He calls everyone he can think of who can help him, explains his situation, and listens to their suggestions. Within three months, he has established many credible contacts, and the law office's telephone is ringing frequently. His superiors have told him that much new business has come into the office, with most of the clients mentioning that they had heard about Hal from a friend of a friend of a friend. Hal has used his networking abilities to generate the new business and is well on his way to establishing a reputation as a "take charge" attorney who can draw clients in by his prestige, a first step to becoming a partner. Coupled with his excellent courtroom technique, good legal knowledge, and hard work, this reputation has the senior partners giving serious thought to including Hal among their number. It probably won't be long now.

WHAT IS NETWORKING?

Networking. What do you think of when you hear the term **networking**? Since this is a relatively new term (around for about only a decade), there has not been time for one definition to become widely accepted. In fact, networking is a term that Humpty Dumpty would love, since it can mean whatever you want it to mean.

"When I use a quote," Humpty Dumpty said in rather a scornful tone," it means just what I choose it to mean—neither more nor less."

"The question is," said Alice, "whether you *can* make a word mean so many different things."

"The question is," said Humpty Dumpty, "which is to be master—that's all."

Humpty's right. How the term is defined tells a lot about the individual defining it. Let's look at a few examples.

> *"Networking is being able to help or benefit from individuals you directly have a relationship with to achieve life's ends."*
>
> PAUL DROLSON
> *Division Manager*
> *American Express, San Diego, California.*

> *"Networking is finding that friendly voice that will talk you through a concern you have."*
>
> GARY ROBERTSON
> *President*
> *International Customer Service Association 1988–1989*
> *Managing Director, Bob Wason & Associates.*

"Activity is the life blood of a successful selling process. Networking is probably the most effective way of creating activity."

JAMES F. LEWIN
Senior Vice President
Security Pacific National Bank, Los Angeles, California.

"We can be walking encyclopedias of knowledge, and yet go to the grave with the music still within ourselves, unless we can master the art of networking. With our changing values, shifting methods, and increasing competition, we find networking far more important than ever before. We must circulate if we expect to percolate. And we must make contacts if we expect to make contracts."

CAVETT ROBERT, CPAE
Chairman Emeritus, National Speakers' Association.

Everyone has his or her own definition of networking. Lynne looked at networking as a tool, as a means to an end, not the end itself. To her networking meant gathering and collecting, and gaining information and contacts. In the second case, Hal defined networking as an end, not a means. He wanted solid results not information: clients. "We see networking as a sales technique. It lets us sell ourselves in a professional manner. We used our contacts to meet people who wanted our services."

What does networking mean to you? The following exercise can help you understand its role in your own life.

EXERCISE

List your very first job. Describe how you got it. (Was it a job you had as a teenager? Did your mother, father, or family friend help you obtain it?) State specifically how you networked to get the position.

List your three most recent jobs, last one first. Describe how you obtained them. Trace back as far as you can, going down the chain link by link. For example, even if you got your job through a head hunter—an executive search firm—someone told you about the head hunter. Perhaps you were introduced to your boss by a former coworker. Maybe you used to work for a competitor's firm, and met your current boss in the course of business.

Examples

In 1976, Bettie was selected as Teacher-of-the-Year. In fulfilling responsibilities of that award, she was invited to present a keynote address at a conference in New York City. There she met author and university professor Dr. Louis Ruben. Impressed with Bettie's speech, he invited her to lead a workshop session at a conference he was sponsoring in Chicago in December, 1977. While doing that workshop, Bettie met Thomas Arcienga, a Dean at San Diego State University. Arcienga complimented Bettie on her presentation and said he would like to have her meet Dr. Ray Latta, Department Chair of Administration at SDSU. Dr. Latta later invited Bettie to teach a summer school course at SDSU the following summer. This networking chain was completed when the University's president, conducting a national search to fill a professorial position, invited Bettie to apply for that full-time position. In 1980, Bettie was appointed as professor in Administration/ Leadership, and moved to San Diego to assume that tenured post. Louis Ruben had been the *key networking* link in Bettie's position. While at the university, she authored several articles, which led to a contract with a major publisher to write a book. It was through this book that she met Brian Tracy, President of the Institute for Executive Development, eventually leading to an executive post with that company.

In 1984, Anne was attending the National Speakers Association National Convention in Washington, DC. On the final banquet night, she forgot something in her room and left her table mates to go back to get the information. She got on the elevator, and in her networking communication style, reached out and said, "Hi, I'm Anne Boe. I'm in career management and networking. What do you do?"

The gentleman on the elevator said, "Oh. I see you are a speaker. I am not a speaker; I write about speakers." Anne never talked so fast between Floor 1 and Floor 10 in her entire speaking career! The man on the elevator was Jeff Waddle, Publishing Editor for *Meeting Magazine* for Meeting Planners International. By the time she reached the tenth floor, they had exchanged business cards. He had told her that his national convention would be in Phoenix in six months, and would turn her materials over to his meeting planner, Mary Hammond. Mary was the Educational Director for Meeting Planners International.

Anne, six months later, did an educational session for Meeting Planners International and was asked to return the following year when the international conference was held in San Diego. She was then asked by the new Education Director, Karen Hodges, to keynote the Miami conference, and speak on networking. In her audience, at the Miami conference, was Karen Peterson from Tupperware Home Parties. Karen Peterson took Anne Boe's information to her boss, Fran Watkins, and Anne, in August of 1988, keynoted seven Tupperware Jubilees and spoke to 18,000 people during that month. Networking has definitely paid off in Anne's career.

After You Have Completed the Exercise . . .

The goal of the exercise is to make you think of how common networking is in your own life, how often you use it without perhaps being aware of doing so. You have networks of your own (personal and professional) and are part of the networks of others. (More will be discussed about these topics in Chapters 3 and 4.) A network is not an entity; it is a changing process. It is what you make of it. As you go through the book, your definition of a network will probably change several times. You will catch yourself saying, "Ah, I never thought of that! Yes, I do network like that, but I never really considered it networking." You might think, "Hmm, that's a good point. I could do that myself. I can use this networking strategy to get what I want, to meet my goals."

NETWORKING TODAY

Networking, under many different names, has been around as long as people have needed to barter. People have always used their contacts to get what they wanted. Networking is a dynamic, ever-changing process. The skill won't be obsolete in a few years because it's not just the latest buzzword or industry jargon. This means that networking is an activity that must be maintained. You cannot simply say, "Well, that's it. We have created our network; it's in place!" Networking is not a one-time task, but a constant technique, an ongoing process.

In our years of networking, we have come up with ten critical rules that we think are the foundation of this essential skill. We present them below, each illustrated with a brief example. As you read through these, think about whether you follow these rules in your own business or personal networks.

1. BE OPENMINDED

This is perhaps the cardinal rule of networking. Networking is an on-going process that can touch all aspects of your life. Personal and professional contacts have a way of coming together to expand your resources.

Jason considers himself a skilled networker. He has a large Rolodex®, neatly cross-indexed, with names and numbers and brief descriptions of people in different fields. He believes

that in just a few minutes he can access the name and number
of a person in nearly any field.

Last weekend, Jason's wife, a reporter, took him to a
professional cartoonists' convention she was covering. Jason
had a wonderful time, meeting the cartoonists and laughing
until he hurt at their jokes and stories about what they really
wanted to put in their strips but were prevented from doing so
by eagle-eyed editors. He noticed that some people were exchanging cards, though he didn't. "I was having such a great
time that I wanted to keep on exchanging jokes, not cards. Besides, I am an architect. I couldn't see how my field could have
any relation to that of cartooning. As far as I was concerned,
I was having a very pleasant afternoon, nothing more. Making
business contacts never entered my mind."

A few weeks after the convention, Jason got a visit
from a broker who often introduced him to people who were
considering custom-built homes. "The broker told me that
her prospective client was interviewing several architects for
what would be a big and highly remunerative job. It turned
out that the client was a freelance humorist. My first reaction
was 'Great, we'll have contacts in common, I can drop a few
names and get the job.' Then I realized that I hadn't exchanged
cards with anyone, and in fact had not really bothered getting
names straight. I might have met someone at the convention
who knew the client, or maybe even met the client himself,
but I'd never know. I lost the job to another architect who
had recently completed a project nearby. But, you know, I still
wonder whether I could have gotten the job if I had done some
networking that weekend, instead of thinking that I already
had a solid enough network to ignore any fresh input. I won't
make that mistake again."

There may be any number of reasons Jason didn't get
the job. However, in the back of his mind, he will always wonder whether maybe, just maybe, a little judicious name dropping or having several mutual contacts might have gotten him
the contract. Have you ever found yourself in that position,
brooding over regrets after the fact? Have you ever passed up
the opportunity to exchange business cards, to network, only
to feel later that you made a mistake? Many of us have had

this experience. Perhaps we have made the mistake of feeling we already have strong, full networks. Don't close the door. Keep working at the art of networking. You never know when the card you collect so casually today will lead to something important tomorrow.

2. BE PREPARED

"Success is when preparedness meets opportunity."—Joe D. Batten. It doesn't do much good to be *willing* to network if you are not *prepared* to do so. Some ways to be prepared are obvious, like having enough business cards or brochures when you need them. Other aspects are less obvious. For example, when you go to a function, professional or personal, do you take a few minutes beforehand to think about what you want to get out of the function in terms of networking and what you are willing to give? Shirley did, with positive results.

Shirley owns a temporary office help business, sending out stenographers, computer operators, and the like to offices on a daily basis. She is always looking for additional workers. One weekend she was at a mall for lunch when she noticed one store had a "Young Marrieds" bridal fair slated for the next weekend. She went to the fair, reasoning that there would be a lot of women there who might be considering part-time work. "I was right. I walked around a little at first, introducing myself and talking about what I was looking for and what I could offer. Soon, I was surrounded. I felt like the most popular exhibit at the fair, as everyone was asking for my card and wanting to know how she could get in touch with me to explore job opportunities. My networking paid off that day in the number of inquiries I got and the potential employees I gave my card to. And who knows how many of those women will pass along my card or tell others about me as well?"

Shirley was successful in meeting her goals because she was ready, willing, and able to network. In this case, her imagination allowed her to use her networking skills in an unusual place—a bridal fair.

3. TREAT THOSE IN YOUR NETWORK AS EQUALS

Networks are different from bureaucracies. In a bureaucracy, there is a hierarchy, a ranking. You may have a salesclerk in your network as well as a nuclear physicist. Remember, everyone is equal in the eyes of a Rolodex.

Murray just finished getting his Ph.D. in chemistry. While he was going through school, he spent a lot of time in the lab, teaching and assisting. As soon as he was awarded his degree, he took a prestigious job with a large firm. His old associates at the lab were afraid that he would ignore them, but Murray made a point of keeping in touch. He called regularly, met them once a month for lunch, and clipped and sent them articles from his company newsletter that he knew would interest them. Whatever contact he had with his old associates was on an equal footing. His new colleagues teased Murray over spending time "in the old neighborhood." They reminded him that it was more important to his career to cultivate those above him.

One day, Murray's new firm was awarded a large contract. The money was excellent, but in estimating the bid someone had made a mistake in calculating the manpower and resources the job would take. The firm found itself without enough people to do the work, and without enough lab space and equipment to accommodate any new personnel. Murray, after a few calls to his old friends, went into his boss's office with a proposal. The extra work could be subcontracted to the other lab, where men and women with whom Murray had worked before would do an excellent job on it. Murray's boss listened as Murray went through his offer point by point: The other technicians were available, were willing to do the work, were qualified, and could use their own lab. Murray himself could work closely with them; since they were all used to each other's ways, there would be little time wasted explaining matters or getting accustomed to different techniques. When Murray left the office, he had the congratulations of his boss ringing in his ears. His colleagues at the new firm—who had not bothered to keep in touch with their old contacts—learned an important lesson about the value of networking.

Murray reaped the benefits of following the **equals** rule. He worked at keeping in touch with those he once worked with even though now he might be considered "beyond them!" Because he had kept in touch, he was able to make a quick offer and back it up with the people to do the work. Perhaps he saved the project for the company. At the very least, he elevated himself in the eyes of his boss. A good payoff for keeping in touch!

4. CHOOSE MEMBERS BASED ON INFORMATION, NOT POSITION

The goal of networking is to share and acquire information. You want to know something: who can get a task done, who has the real power in an organization, and so on. Down the road, you may have a secondary goal of getting more than information (remember for example that Hal the attorney used networking to get clients, not just information), but in most instances, your network's primary value is as a source of referrals and information. Therefore, be certain that when you select a person for inclusion in your network (and that process is not as pretentious as it sounds: It could be as simple as slipping the individual's card into your wallet, or putting his or her name on your organizer) you do so based on the information the person has not his or her position.

Melanie decided that she needed to network better than she had been doing. Her first task was to go through her file and discard all the information on secretaries, salesclerks, and others whom she considered the "rank and file." From now on, she was only going to have presidents, CEOs, and other executives in her network. She stopped calling and meeting with her former contacts and spent all her time pouring through books and corporate statements to find the names of those in the upper positions, then scheming about how to get an introduction to such people.

Melanie's car had been giving her problems for months. She finally decided it was time to get another, but could only afford a used car. Having heard many horror stories about used cars, and being fully aware of the paucity of her knowledge about auto mechanics ("I'm a real estate salesperson; what do I know about cars?"), she decided to hire someone to check out the cars she was interested in. She needed someone who had the time to go to the houses of those who advertised their cars (Melanie would read the ads and circle the ones that looked promising within her price range) and do a mechanical check.

"I thought I could use my network to get the information I wanted. Unfortunately, everyone I called was in such a high position that he never even considered having a used car. People were really kind, wanting to help, but could do no more than refer me to their Mercedes or BMW dealerships. I could have called them myself. What I wanted was the name of someone who had already done the work for my contact, someone that my contact knew personally and trusted. After all, I was going to trust my life to a car checked over by the mechanic; I wanted a mechanic I could trust. I called everyone I could think of, but no one had the information I wanted. Finally, I went back into my files and dug out an old telephone log that had the number of a secretary on it. I called her. She had a few things to say about how I had been ignoring her (I'm ashamed to say that I hadn't even returned her calls) but did give me the information I wanted. She and several of her friends all had used cars and recommended a young man to do the check for me. I called him and he worked out perfectly. I learned a lesson: higher ranking is not always better informed."

5. DON'T BE AFRAID TO ASK

There you are, with a strong network. You have kept an open mind and been flexible and accumulated a huge card file of names, numbers, and descriptions of people who could help you. Now you need help but are too shy or embarrassed to ask for it.

Casey has decided to get back into the job market after taking time off to raise a family. She worked for years in the marketing department of a large firm, but finds out when she asks to be rehired that there are no openings. After answering what seems like every want ad in the Sunday *Times*, Casey is discouraged. "No one wants to hire someone like me, older and out of touch with the market. I know I could get back into the swing of things quickly, if I only have a chance. But who is going to give me that chance?"

A friend of Casey's tells her about a job as a part-time receptionist at a health spa. At first Casey feels that the job is beneath her, and that it would not propel her towards her final goal of reentering marketing. However, the friend convinces her that working at something—anything—for right now, will improve her skills and help her during a future interview ("Why yes, I am working in customer relations at the Ed Gains Health Spa"). Casey gets the job, and soon finds herself enjoying not only the work but also the contact with many people. "I sign up new members, help others with problems, chat to a lot of business people every day. I've gotten to know some of the regulars pretty well and have told them about my job hunt. They have given me their business cards, and say to call if they can help. A few have even promised to keep an eye out for a job for me. But of course, I don't take their promises seriously, I know that I have said things like that in the past, 'Sure, call anytime, glad to help!' without really meaning it. These people are just being kind. They don't really mean it. Why should they help the person who just checks their membership cards and signs them in?"

Casey is breaking two rules of networking. First, she is not using her resources. Here she has several people offering to help, and she is ignoring them. Even if a few of them are just spouting expected platitudes, there is always the chance that others sincerely mean the offers. It only takes one. Second, Casey is breaking the previous rule about equality. By being afraid that she is viewed only as a receptionist, she forgets that in a network all people are equal. This, incidentally, is more common than people realize. Many people become discouraged and depressed after losing a job or spending weeks looking for a new position. They have been rejected so much that they feel there must be something wrong with them. After all, everyone else has a good job; why not they? Casey has fallen into having this mind set as well. By thinking of herself as unworthy of help, she is squandering a wealth of opportunity.

6. DON'T WASTE YOUR RESOURCES

This rule is a variation on rule 5. Rule 5 warned you not to let your resources go to waste by being unused. This rule reminds you not to use resources *the wrong way.* You can abuse the members of your network only once—after that you may find that they make themselves unavailable to you.

Steve had a large network of professional contacts which he used constantly. If a person he met just that day mentioned in passing, "Someday, I'm going to have to think about working on my financial portfolio," Steve would call three or four financial planners in his portfolio and give them the man's name. If an acquaintance at a party said casually that he was thinking about getting some help for his daughter who had a reading problem, Steve would give the acquaintance's name to several teachers he knew who were in the tutoring business.

Steve thought he was networking skillfully and effectively. Therefore, he was surprised and hurt when several of his contacts asked him point blank not to give out their names anymore. "Well, that's gratitude for you! Here I break my neck to get them business, and they throw it back in my face." Ah, but was he really getting them business? No. What happened was different.

When Steve would call his network contacts, the conversation would go like this:

"Hey, Frank! Steve Ciera here. I know you are a financial planner, and I have a really hot prospect for you. The man's name is Tony Pradi and his telephone number is 555-2121. He is really eager to make a complete shuffle, invest heavily. I think this is a live one, and you should call him right away."

Naturally, the listener would thank Steve profusely, then call the prospective client right away, only to hear, "Who? Steve Ciera? Uh, yeah, I know him, but not really well. We were just introduced a few days ago. Financial planning? I, uh, think I, uh, might have mentioned that I want to redo my portfolio sometime, but nothing definite. I certainly didn't want to do anything right now. I didn't give what's-his-name, Steve, my number. He must have gotten it somewhere else. And he didn't mention you to me. Who did you say you are again?"

Of course, Frank feels like a fool. First, the "hot prospect" isn't any such thing. He isn't interested in Frank's services; he had only made an off-the-cuff comment. Second, Steve doesn't really know the prospect and didn't get permission to give out his number. And third, the prospect had no idea who Frank was, not having been briefed by Steve ahead of time. Frank wound up wasting his time and feeling sheepish. Do you wonder that he would ask Steve not to do him any favors anymore?

Steve wasted two resources, Frank and the prospective client. Frank is annoyed and irritated; the prospective client probably thinks Steve had some nerve to give out the information. Of course, Steve is the injured innocent in his own mind. He sincerely feels that he did a favor for two people, bringing them together to their mutual advantage. He hasn't learned the lesson of being discriminating in how he uses his network.

7. GIVE WITHOUT EXPECTATION

Although you do hope to reap some reward somewhere down the line, don't make doing so the only reason you network. Share your information gladly, without always questioning, "And now, what's in it for me?" If you give of yourself only because you expect something in return, you leave yourself open for disappointment and can cause ill will between you and another member of your network.

David, an optometrist, got a call from an acquaintance of his who wanted information on a new surgical procedure. The friend, Jim, made it clear that he needed the information so he could pass it along to a friend. David spent quite a bit of time talking with Jim, explaining the procedure, and followed up by sending him some literature. Then David sat back and waited for the quid pro quo, the "something for something," or return. When nothing happened, he became upset and annoyed. "I can't believe I got nothing out of this. Doesn't the man realize I spent time getting him what he wanted? I even gave him the number of another associate of mine who also spoke with him." A couple of months later, when Jim called again, David was curt and abrupt with him. A few minutes into the conversation, it was clear that Jim had called just to say hello, not to offer any reward for David's past help. David closed the conversation quickly, leaving Jim wondering what had happened.

Though it may seem as if Jim is in error here, it is David who is closing the doors to a future relationship of 'this ones for you.' Remember, a return favor may not come back to you immediately, *but*, eventually it will. Be patient. In the meantime, be generous with your help and support.

8. SAY THANK YOU

Express your appreciation. If someone is helping you via net-working, be certain you let him or her know how much you appreciate it. You can say thank you verbally, casually. You can give your thanks with a small gift, if appropriate, or with a remembrance. One of the best ways we have found to say thanks is to tell the helper the outcome of the help.

Mary Jane called Don. "Hi Don, if you have a minute, I would love to pick your brain. I am anticipating bidding for a job in East County and need to know whether you have had any experience with the city council member from that area." Don laughed, and said Mary Jane should come in to see him. Don told Mary Jane all about the rather cantankerous council member, what experiences he had had with him, and how best to get around or deal with his idiosyncracies. Mary Jane thanked Don, and left. But a month later she followed up with a long letter. In it, she told Don all about her meeting with the councilman, and made a humorous story out of the encounter. She ended by saying that she did in fact get the job, and thanking Don again.

Don felt appreciated. He had accepted Mary Jane's thanks at the time of the meeting and never really expected to hear anything more about it. When he got the follow-up letter, he was pleased that Mary Jane had taken the time to tell him the outcome. He was eager to help Mary Jane again.

9. SET REALISTIC AND ACHIEVABLE GOALS

No one else is going to do all of your work for you. No one, no matter how good a contact he or she may be, is going to be able to make things work out perfectly. You are in control of your own life; in the long run, only you make the decisions and take the steps that determine how successful and productive your life is.

Belinda had worked for years as a schoolteacher, running a math lab at an elementary school. The school was closed down under a budget cut, and Belinda found herself out of work. She enjoyed the leisure for three years, then decided it was time to get back into the business world. She didn't want to work in education any more, and thought that "business sounds good. After all, I have had experience managing people, and was the head of the entire math lab program. Surely those skills can transfer over into another are. I'm not sure exactly what I should do yet, but I can be a good catch for some enterprising company that appreciates me."

Knowing that her friend Wanda worked for a large corporation as a software quality-control engineer, Belinda asked for Wanda's help in getting a job. Out of friendship Wanda agreed to write a letter saying that Belinda was a hard worker and intelligent, well-organized, and motivated. Wanda also arranged a meeting between Belinda and the personnel director at Wanda's corporation. Belinda went to the meeting positive that she now had an in with the company and would certainly get the job. She was ready to start discussing salary and utterly devastated when the personnel director turned her down. "He said that I didn't have the qualifications or experience for any job in the firm. But he should have known that I could handle anything, I mean with some training. After all, my friend Wanda recommended me, and she is highly thought of in her company."

Belinda had two unrealistic goals. First, secure in her self-confidence that she was an intelligent, hard-working woman, she assumed that she could take on a job for which she was unqualified. She knew little about the business world and believed that a person's motivation was more important than her qualifications or abilities. Coming from the field of education, Belinda was accustomed to hearing, "You can do this job, with just a little more education and training." It did not occur to her that firms are more interested in hiring someone who already knows the job than a neophyte, no matter how eager she is.

Second, Belinda had expected that merely getting a reference and an introduction to the personnel director ensured her a job. (She did not even notice that Wanda's very carefully written letter mentioned admirable character traits, but blatantly omitted discussing experience or qualification.) She did not accept responsibility for her own life in setting a realistic and achievable job procurement goal.

Belinda had set two unrealistic goals. First, she wanted a job for which she was unqualified. Second, she had expected that merely getting a reference or introduction from a networking colleague would get her the job. She did not take responsibility for setting a realistic and achievable goal.

10. BE COMMITTED AND DETERMINED TO DO WHATEVER IT TAKES

Networking requires commitment and patience. It is an ongoing process. You cannot build good networking relationships instantly; they take time to develop. In addition, you need to be determined. Not everyone is going to be eager to be a part of your network, thrilled to lend a helping hand. You may have to work at joining or developing a network.

Ruth went to three meetings of the Professional Woman's Association, handed out her cards, joined in conversations, and went home waiting for the telephone to ring. Much to her surprise, no one called to network. Therefore Ruth thought she would begin. She telephoned several people whom she had met and was surprised to find that they were not eager to spend time chatting with her on the telephone. They all made it clear that they were busy and wanted to her to get to the point. When Ruth did make her request—a reference for her daughter who wanted to join the job market—they turned her down. As one woman put it, "Ruth, I barely know you and I don't know your daughter at all. How can I help you?"

Ruth was disappointed, and told her daughter that networking just plain didn't work. "I tried, but it didn't work for me."

Perhaps it was natural for Ruth to be disappointed, but she might have given up too quickly. Networking takes time and effort. It was not fair of her to expect one brief meeting to result in everything she wanted. If we were advising Ruth, we would tell her to keep working at networking. The relationships are new and take time to develop. Continue going to meetings, doing favors for others, becoming more well-known. Slowly, bring the daughter into the conversations, talking about her accomplishments until others feel as if they know her themselves from having heard so much about her. That way, they will be more comfortable giving her help later on. The moral of the story is to be patient and persistent.

NETWORKING IN THE FUTURE

We have given you our definition of networking today, and ten important rules we have developed over years of networking and helping others do the same. Now that you have learned these rules, can you sit back and feel you have matters under control? Sorry, no. We want to emphasize that networking is ever changing. Therefore, one of the thoughts in your mind should be, "How can I know *today* what networking will be like *tomorrow,* so that I can be planning and preparing?" Of course, no one can tell exactly what the future of anything will be. Who would have predicted the mass popularity of calculators and computers just a generation ago? Who would have thought that the gas stations that enticed customers with dish giveaways ("Fill 'er up and get a mug free!") would have to turn customers away? Who would have thought that business schools would have among the highest enrollment of any colleges in the universities? Maybe you couldn't have made any of those predictions, but someone did.

There are always those few people who seem to know what the future will be like and who act on their knowledge or predictions. People who invested in Apple Computers or oil stocks at the right time made a pretty penny. Students who got their Ph.D.'s in business ten years ago are faculty members in demand at many schools across the country. It is no secret that knowledge is power. It is therefore important that you have some knowledge of where networking is going, what it will be like in five, ten, twenty-five years. While we offer no magic absolutes, there are some trends from which we can make the following predictions.

1. NETWORKING WILL BECOME A HIRING POINT

Employers may ask prospective employees to take exams about networking, or to demonstrate through role-playing their ability to network. Some people in the service fields take their clients with them (Hairdressers who move from one salon to another often answer classified ads that say, "Stylist wanted, with own following"; professionals often have client lists, like stockbrokers or advertising executives who bring loyal clients with them to their new firms or editors in publishing houses might take their authors); employers may ask for lists of clients or contacts and judge job applicants based on such lists.

2. NETWORKING WILL BE ESSENTIAL TO CREATE VISIBILITY WITHIN PROFESSIONAL ORGANIZATIONS

Many large organizations today can be impersonal. It is easy to get lost in the crowd. Yet if you know how to network, soon everyone knows you. You become the person in the know, a lynchpin for the group. In order to gain the most from your membership in the group, good networking skills are essential.

3. NETWORKING WILL BE RECOGNIZED AS AN IMPORTANT BUSINESS SKILL AND TAUGHT IN TRAINING PROGRAMS

Large and small firms will include courses and seminars in networking in their training programs. Some firms already have games-playing activities in which the trainee is asked "What would you do if. . . ." Networking programs would be similar, asking, "Where would you go to get the following information?" or "How would you go about finding out . . . ?"

4. NETWORKING WILL BE TAUGHT IN BUSINESS SCHOOLS

It was not very long ago that business schools emphasized only the solid or quantitative subjects like statistics, finance, and economics. In the last few decades, soft or qualitative courses have been introduced. Courses like Management of Organizations and Organizational Behavior have a psychology flavor to them and are gaining more and more acceptance in business schools nationwide, becoming part of a core course at many. Networking will become either a part of such qualitative courses, or (more probably) an entire course by itself. Business education is, after all, a pragmatic field. Schools are careful to teach those skills that are used in and demanded by businesses. If the business world learns to value networking skills (as mentioned in the first point), business schools will soon get the message and offer courses teaching and testing networking skills.

5. NETWORKING WILL BECOME MORE FORMALIZED

You may not know how many formal and informal networks of which you are a part. As networking becomes a more recognized and appreciated skill, that may all change. Just as you know that you are considered a client of a dentist because she or he sends you regular checkup notices and you remember you are insured with Company X because your agent sends you birthday and Christmas cards, you may soon find yourself getting billet-doux from those who want you in their networks. Lynne has already heard from a man who sent her a card in the mail saying, "I am establishing a network of professionals who might be interested in working with relocated families. May I add your name to the list? I will be calling you in the next week to discuss the matter with you." Lynne has never met the sender of the card, but she spoke with him and let her name be put on the sender's network list.

6. NETWORKING WILL BEOME MORE DISCRIMINATORY AND SPECIALIZED

Long ago, there were unclassified ads. Ads offering puppies were side by side with ads soliciting petition distributors. Lonely hearts ads asking Muffin to call her Big Boy were next to announcements that the circus would be in town in a month. Those who had a specific need had to wallow through all the surplus information. They probably got quite an education but may have felt frustrated from wasting time. Papers now have ads classified. We can turn to an index and find the classification we want, then go look under it for what we want. We save time and anguish.

The same may become true of networking. Right now, an axiom of networking is to include *as many* different people as possible. (Remember the architect who regretted not getting cards at the cartoonist convention?) However, as networking becomes more sophisticated, the day may come when it has to be more discriminating and specialized. More remote contacts will be pushed to the back of the card catalog or weeded out completely. If everyone is networking, after all, it will be easy to use one of your more direct contacts to find a remote contact, should the occasion for one arise.

7. PROFESSIONAL NETWORKING ORGANIZATIONS WILL ABOUND

A breakfast club that meets for the express purpose of networking is one type of professional networking organization. But there may be another kind as well. Just as there are professional head hunters and employment counsellors, in the not-too-distant future there will be professional network counsellors. You may get to the office one morning and find that you need to find someone who can give a presentation on the implications of a proposed new tax law. Rather than picking up the phone and calling your friends and professional associates to get a name, you look in the Yellow Pages for the number of a professional networking association. You explain your situation to the dulcet voice on the other end of the line. Either in a moment over the phone, or within a few days in the mail, you will get a list of highly recommended people. Probably that list will discuss not only the individuals and their qualifications but also the people who referred the workers into the network and the comments other networkers have made about them.

These professional organizations can work several different ways. Some might be free to the users, getting their money at the other end from the referral fees. Some might charge per question or piece of information. Others might be subscribed to by the firm, so that you can call as often as you like. Some of the more forward-thinking businesses might establish their own in-house networking associations. Did you ever see the movie *Desk Set* with Katherine Hepburn and Spencer Tracy? Ms. Hepburn worked in an in-house reference department for a large firm. Workers would call her with information they needed for their project; in a few moments she would find the answers. The same could be true with networking. One worker could supply names and information about a variety of topics.

8. NETWORKING WILL KEEP COMPETITIVE BUSINESSES IN BUSINESS

Getting together to get ahead will be highly valued in business. It is rare that any one industry or firm completely monopolizes a particular field. With many different companies working in one area, firms must cooperate to survive. Those companies and individuals who know how to get together to get ahead will be successful; those who suspiciously practice isolationism and refuse to network will soon be driven out.

9. NETWORKING RELATIONSHIPS WILL DETERMINE BUSINESS PROFITABILITY

This idea is somewhat related to the previous one. Those firms who know how to network, who can cooperate rather than compete with other companies, will achieve greater profits. Remember the wonderful movie, *Miracle on 34th Street,* in which Macy's and Gimbels broke tradition by cooperating rather than competing? Both firms ended up having the greatest Christmas profits ever.

10. NETWORKING WILL BE ESSENTIAL FOR CREATING BALANCE, PROFESSIONALLY AND PERSONALLY

It is difficult to keep a strong and healthy personal life when you are working hard, yet doing so is very important to your well-being. Networking helps us do just that. We can use the warm, personal contacts with others in our network to balance the sometimes impersonal aspects of business. We can develop relationships that support establishing realistic and achievable goals. Networking will provide a strong bridge between personal and professional lives.

CONCLUSION

We hope you have been thinking about what networking means to you as you went through this chapter. We gave you our definitions, and the definitions of some of our associates, but remember: Since networking is a skill, it varies from person to person. Not everyone has the same definition, or the same level of talent at networking. One of our goals in this book is to make you aware of the role networking plays in your life, what an important skill it is, so that you can begin to hone that skill. If you are reading this book at a time when you are trying to find a job or eager to shift positions, you may be a little suspicious of something that seems so much effort. Relax. Managing a network is time consuming, but it does pay big dividends. And with the tips giving in this book, you can learn how to manage that network effectively and efficiently, with less time and effort than you might have anticipated.

In this chapter, we introduced ten rules of networking we have developed over our years in business; you may wish to add more of your own. We gazed into our crystal balls and predicted fearlessly that networking will be an even more essential skill in the future. In brief, we tried to share with you some of our feelings and information about networking, because information is power as we will discuss in the next chapter.

2
INFORMATION IS POWER

*J*oan is the branch manager of a large insurance firm. She is a workaholic who feels that she has to be involved in every detail of her job, from making the major decisions to overseeing the smallest choices. Joan overhears one of her secretaries complaining about a typewriter that is "positively antique!" and decides to think about revamping the office. Joan spends all day Friday taking inventory of the office, talking to the workers about their equipment, identifying specific needs that the office has. This task takes all day. Joan feels a little guilty about avoiding her other duties (some of them quite pressing), but reasons that "This is something that has to be done, and if it has to be done, the best way to make sure it is done right is to do it myself." Joan spends a few hours on the telephone getting price quotes from office supply firms. Over the weekend, on her own time, Joan writes a very detailed, professional-looking report just right, because it will have to go to the national headquarters. The amount of money Joan is advocating spending to upgrade the office has to be approved separately, as it is far beyond her office's annual equipment budget.

Joan burns the midnight oil on the weekend, and Federal Expresses the finished document to the national headquarters. The next day, she gets the call she has been expecting from her immediate superior. "Joan, this is an impressive report. I hope you didn't put too much time into it?"

Joan beams. "Well, as a matter of fact, I did. If I do something, I might as well do it right. And this is something that had to be done."

Her boss interjects, "No, it didn't."

Joan is silent for a minute. "I beg your pardon?"

"No, Joan, it didn't have to be done. We have been aware that our branch offices need more modern equipment and have spent the past few weeks addressing the situation. You will hear in a week or two when you may expect the new machines in your own office. I'm sorry you had to waste your time. Well, at least you did it on a weekend, so it didn't interfere with your professional responsibilities."

Joan hangs up and imagines that she must look like a dog who has just lost a bone. "I feel like an absolute fool. Here I put in all that time, did a great report, and all for nothing. I just hope he never finds out that I spent all day Friday on it too. I'd better get busy this week and be sure to catch up on everything I missed that day."

Joan has dinner that night with a friend who is the manager of another branch office of the same insurance firm. She pours out her tale of woe, confidently expecting sympathy. Sid shakes his head. "I wish you had talked this over with me, Joan. I knew about the overhaul plans a few weeks ago, and could have told you."

Joan looks at him. "You knew? How could you know and I not? we get the same reports from the central office. I work as hard as you do. Where did the information come from?"

"Calm down Joan, no one is saying that you don't work hard. And no, I don't have a spy inside the central office to give me information so that I look good. It's very simple, really. I keep in touch with the plant supervisor of my building. I drop by his office every now and then, just to shoot the breeze. He was the one who had heard rumors of the new equipment, and passed them along to me in the course of a casual conversation."

What happened? Joan cheated the company out of a day of her professional services, wasted her own weekend, and looked like a fool to her boss. She felt like an idiot, especially when she found out how simple it could have been to avoid all these problems. It was called networking. Sid networked with the plant supervisor; Joan was more interested in "doing the job right, which means doing it on my own."

George had lunch with his boss yesterday. Over dessert, Ms. Robison mentioned that she wanted to hire someone with robotics experience, an engineer or technician who could start work right away. She had spoken with several employment agencies, but had not been able to get an experienced person, someone with just the right qualifications. Ms. Robison didn't ask George for his help, but as he was listening to her, he was mentally ruffling through his Rolodex. As soon as he got back to the office, he began making calls. A friend of a friend of an associate knew of someone who used to teach robotics at a school in Michigan. Getting the person's number, George called him and found that he was retired, but bored and looking for something to do. With a little interviewing, George discovered that the man's qualifications seemed to be exactly what Ms. Robison wanted. George gave the man Ms. Robison's number.

Later that day, Ms. Robison, a rare smile on her face, dropped by George's office. "George, I want to thank you for telling Dr. Parton about our opening. He seems to be the right person for the job. I didn't expect you to handle personnel for me, and so quickly too. What other talents have you kept hidden from me? I can see I am going to have to involve you more; you were invaluable in helping me fill this position."

Hooray for George! Besides feeling good about himself, George gave his career a push. By making a few telephone calls and using his network, he was able to connect and fill a need. His boss's opinion of him soared. He may be more involved in management in the future; he certainly will be consulted more. He has begun a success cycle. The more he is involved, the more he will be able to help, and the more involved he will become.

Lorna and Gordon are both CPAs for a large tax firm. Each is trying to obtain a promotion. At last week's meeting, their boss mentioned that he had heard rumors about new changes in the tax laws, but couldn't seem to pin anything down. He asked the people at the meeting to use their sources to get any information they could.

Lorna went back to her office and stared at her telephone. She had no network of people whom she could call. She finally resorted to telephoning reference librarians, who knew less than she did. Gordon, on the other hand, flipped through his card index. He found a business card of a Phil Ewing, attorney. Gordon had met Phil on a vacation last year. The two men had had an interesting conversation. Gordon had been able to answer a few questions for Phil, give him a little advice. Phil's last words were, "If I can ever do anything for you, just let me know." Gordon called Phil, reminded him of their previous conversation, and asked for any information he might have. A few hours later, Phil called back with the telephone number of a friend of his who is the business editor of a newspaper in Washington, D.C. Gordon called the man and got the inside scoop. The next day, Gordon was able not only to tell his boss of the proposed changes but also to give him the name of the editor who had passed them along.

Lorna had no network to use. Gordon had one and used it well. Because he had kept an individual's card, he had a name and number to call. Because he had helped the individual, he got help himself. It was a far-reaching network. The boss asked Gordon, Gordon asked Phil, Phil asked the editor, and the editor came through. To complete the cycle, the boss called the editor to confirm the information and to pick the man's brain a bit more. And Gordon? He got an invitation to address the next meeting, an invitation to lunch, and the inside track to the promotion.

Information *is* power. If you know the facts, you can prevent catastrophes or encourage time- and money-saving activities. If you have the right information, you can be in the right place doing the right thing at the right time. If you have good contacts, you can help others who are in positions to help you. You have probably been in positions analogous to those of the people in the above anecdotes. Can you recall the last time you mentally cringed, "Gee, if only I had known that!" Do you remember the last time you sat back, a smug smile on your face, and chortled because you had information, or access to information, that your competition didn't?

WHAT'S THE PROBLEM HERE?

Did you find that identifying the problem in the above scenarios was relatively simple? Good. That's an important skill for you to have when you begin networking. If you want to solve a problem, the first step is to identify the problem. In most instances, a lack of information is obvious. If your boss asks you a question, getting the answer is the problem. If you have to find facts and figures, doing so is the difficulty. However, there are some times when all you have is a vague feeling that something is wrong, that you have forgotten something, that you could be doing something more. If Joan had had that feeling, and reacted to it, she might have saved herself much embarrassment and frustration. We can remember several times when we stopped what we were doing, and wondered, "What are my subconscious and intuition trying to tell me? Something isn't right here, but I'm not sure what it is."

Networking can help you in these situations. If you know what you need, you go to a person for the information. Networking can also be valuable when you are not quite certain what's going on. If you don't know what is wrong with a report you are preparing, you could ask a friend who is a writer to review it. Perhaps she can find the one thing that is nagging at your subconscious. Maybe a coworker will be willing to pass the report on to a friend who is in your field, but removed from your job. That person can criticize your report objectively. Having a bank of people who can give help, even when you don't know what kind of help you need, is what being resourceful is all about.

Let's get down to specifics as far as identifying the problem. Whether it is a single fact you are seeking or a general opinion, you should have in mind *what* you want before you approach someone for help. Ask yourself the following questions *before* you pick up the telephone or begin to write a letter. In fact, keep this page handy to use as a checklist when you begin your information search. It will help you become more organized and focused.

1. Do I want a specific fact? If so, what is it? Is it a number (sales figures), a date (the year a firm was established), a name (the founder of the firm), a location (the site of the next branch office)?

Specific information I want: _____

_____

_____

2. Is it important that the information I get be a hard, concrete fact as opposed to an estimate or an opinion? Do I need precise references, sources from which the information came, chapter and verse?

I will settle for an estimate or a guess. _____

I need precise facts, backed by references. The references or sources are: _____

_____

_____

3. Do I need background information about the person giving the information or the opinion? (In other words, will my boss want me to justify this information by listing the qualifications of the person who presented it?)

Qualifications or information about my personal source: _____

_____

_____

4. Do I want something sent to me or can I learn what I need in a conversation? If I need something sent, how will it be sent (regular mail, overnight courier)? How many copies do I need, and in what form? (Are copies okay, or do I need something more official?)

I need the following information in the following form: _____

_____

_____

5. Should I recompense the supplier of the information in any way? Do I pay for his or her time and effort? How much? When? In what form? How much do I offer for "expenses" (mailing and shipping costs)? What do I do if the person exceeds my budgeted costs; who handles the extra?

I offer the following compensation: _____

_____

_____

6. Is time of the essence? Must I have the information now, or can it be supplied at the other person's convenience?

I need the information by: _____

_____

_____

7. Do I want the other person to take action or just to supply information? Do I need something done?

The action I want taken is: _____

_____

_____

8. Do I want the names and numbers of others who can provide more information? Should I have the original (primary) source contact the secondary source first to ease my path?

I want the primary source to: —————————————

————————————————————————————

Can you see how having all this information written down *before* you ask your questions can help? You look organized, and have a clear idea of what you want and when and in what form. You prevent that foolish feeling we have all experienced when we have to call back again and again with a shamefaced, "Uh, there's something else . . . . " These guidelines can help you as they helped Ellen.

Ellen wanted to get a mailing list of members of an elite club. The club's management will not release the names and addresses of its members. Ellen knows her associate Ray has a sister who belongs to the club. Ellen decides to telephone Ray. She goes through the list to organize her thoughts, knowing that Ray is a busy man who does not like to spend much time on the telephone. Here is how she focuses her thoughts, using the list.

1. SPECIFIC FACTS

I want the names and mailing addresses of the members of the Regina Club. If possible, I'd like the telephone numbers as well, although that is not essential.

2. CONCRETE FACTS

I want the most recent addresses, the current membership list.

3. BACKGROUND INFORMATION

I don't need to know anything about Ray himself. However, it might be good for me to know something about his sister, if only to start a conversation. In reality, though, information about her is not important.

4. TRANSPORTATION

The list will be too long to be read over the telephone. I would like to have it mailed to me. A copy is fine. I will send Ray's sister a self-addressed, stamped envelope. She can send the list by regular mail.

5. COMPENSATION

I can send Ray's sister the cost to cover any copying fees.

6. TIME

I would like the information as soon as possible. There is no deadline, but the earlier I get the information, the better.

7. ACTION

Ray's sister does not need to do anything other than send me the list. I don't expect her to call her fellow members.

8. ADDITIONAL

All I want is the list. I don't need anything else. Ray's sister doesn't have to make any calls or send any letters on my behalf.

WHO'S ON FIRST?

With the above exercise, you determined *what* you need. The next step is to find out *who* can give it to you. Often, these steps occur simultaneously (as you think of what you need, you decide whom to ask). Sometimes, however, you know exactly what you want, but have no idea whom to ask for help. Rather than floundering about, take an organized approach, like the following.

Identify the General Field the Helper Should Be in, or the Qualification Needed

If you have already decided *what* you need, you can project the type of person who can help. For example, if you need someone to give you a mailing list of an organization, you find someone who belongs to that organization. If you'd like to hear the rumors that are going around about tax credits, you want to speak with an accountant or tax attorney. If you want someone to make a speech on your behalf, you need someone who is skilled in your field as well as a competent speaker. If you are really at a loss, totally blank as to whom to call, why not make a list of these qualifications? Think of it as a job description. You have a job that needs to be done; specify the type of person who can do it. As you read the list, you might find a person's name leaping to the forefront of your mind. Or, you might be able to eliminate some people from consideration. Elimination is just as important as selection, allowing you to save yourself time and effort and perhaps money. You also prevent yourself from wasting the time of, and annoying, an obviously unable-to-help individual you might otherwise contact.

Usually, knowing *what* you want, having gone through the list given earlier, will be enough for you to list the person's qualifications. If it is not, try the following.

1. TECHNICAL EXPERTISE

What specific background knowledge or skills does the person need? (Must he or she be able to program a computer or simply use canned software? Must she or he be able to do your taxes or simply give you information about tax shelters?)

2. LICENSES AND CREDENTIALS

What specific legal documents does the individual need? (Does he or she need teaching credentials? A pilot's license?)

3. COST

How expensive can the person be? (Can you pay a large lump sum or a small hourly wage? Can you pay in something other than money, like trading services?)

4. LOCATION

Does the person have to be in a certain place? Is the task geographically oriented? (Can the person write the report anywhere, or will he or she have to use a specific computer located in your building?)

5. AVAILABILITY/TIMING

Does the person have to be available at a specific time or on a specific date? (Can he or she do the task leisurely, or must it be done by a certain date? Is time of the essence? Is this person one who is usually booked weeks in advance?)

You can probably think of more qualifications that are important to you. They will vary with the situation. *Suggestion:* As you become more skilled at networking, keep track of the reasons a person did *not* work out. For example, if you asked a person to do something that his health did not permit, jot down *health* as a qualification. The next time you are considering whom to contact to ask for help, you can add it to your list of things to consider.

Okay, you have identified *what* you need and written a specific description of *who* might be able to do what you want, help you out. Unfortunately, you don't know any such person. What now? Now you ask for help from those whom you do know.

1. TALK, TALK, TALK

Don't be shy about telling others what you are looking for. You have probably done something like this all your life. When you were a teenager and wanted a second-hand car, you asked everyone you knew to keep an eye open for something cheap in running condition. When you wanted a part-time summer job, your parents probably pestered their friends until someone thought of a job opening that would be perfect for you. If you don't get the word out, no one will ever know that her secretary has a friend who could be just the person you need. Go to lunch with people. Talk to people in the parking lot. Hang around the copy machine, looking for people to buttonhole. Tell the office gossip, and make his day by telling him you'd be grateful if he'd talk to as many people as possible. Make telephone calls to people who seem to be sociable, those who are at the center of any office intrigue, those who are the ones we always count on to make the office party a success. Keep talking and letting everyone know what you need.

2. PUT IT IN WRITING

Get the word out on the printed page. Of course, getting things in writing can take longer than communicating them verbally, but if you have the time and need help *now*, this is a good way to go. Is there a company newsletter? Get your request put in

there. Is there a bulletin board? Put your notice on the board:
"Wanted: Someone who can help me get a list of the .... " Many
firms now have computer link-ups, electronic bulletin boards.
Put your message on there daily. You might circulate a memo.
One woman we know, after trying everything else, wrote a flier
and put it on the cars in the parking lot. She got several calls,
including one that put her in touch with the person who was
perfect for the job. The moral of the story is *Get the word out
where it can be seen by the right people,* or by as many people
as possible.

3. USE PROFESSIONAL SOURCES

Reference librarians at central branch libraries are very resourceful. They seem to know everything, and are delighted to
help. They have heard all sorts of requests. A reference librar-
ian might be able to tell you about an organization or club that
has members with the qualifications you are looking for. You
should also use contacts at your monthly professional meetings.

4. FREQUENT OR FORM NETWORKING ORGANIZATIONS

Networking has come out of the closet. It is one of those activities that everyone has always done, but few people have
given a name or talked about specifically. That is all changing.
There are organizations that are professional "matchmakers."
We know of people who belong to groups that were founded
solely to get together different types of people. One such organization, at its last meeting, noted that there were a doctor, nursery operator, teacher, homemaker, writer, salesperson, broker, professor, attorney, television camera operator,
and electrician in just one chattering group alone. If you don't
have a networking organization around you, begin one of your

own. Helpful advice on how to do so is given throughout this book.

Trinh, a salesman, needs someone who can give him an introduction to the owner of a large computer firm. The owner is notorious for not seeing strangers. The only way anyone can get to Mr. Steinfeld is with an introduction from a person Mr. Steinfeld already knows and trusts personally or professionally. Since the computer firm is large and spends much money, those salespeople who call on Steinfeld jealously guard their connection. The few whom Trinh approached said that they were not going to take the chance of losing business with Steinfeld by introducing him to Trinh. Trinh comes to you for help. "I want to meet Mr. Steinfeld. Can you tell me of anyone who can—and is willing to—introduce us?"

What do you do? You begin by having Trinh isolate exactly what he wants. It is not enough to say that he wants an introduction. What kind of introduction? Will he settle for a letter sent on his behalf, a call talking about him? Does he need a face-to-face introduction?

What is Trinh willing to exchange for the favor of the introduction? What, in other words, can he offer to the individual who goes out on a limb and takes Trinh to Steinfeld? Does he have a source that he can share in return?

Finally, you get the preliminaries out of the way. You find that Trinh wants a face-to-face introduction in a business setting (in Steinfeld's own office, if possible). He wants an appointment, not just a chance, quick meeting. Trinh is willing to accompany another salesperson on a routine call. He does not insist that there be a meeting set up for the express purpose of introducing him to Steinfeld.

Trinh is so eager to meet Steinfeld that he is promising virtually anything to the person who will effect the introduction. "You find out what the person wants, and I'll do my best to do it for him. If I have anyone he wants to meet, I'll introduce him. I might even be able to swing a little business his way from one of my own clients."

Now you know what Trinh wants and what he is willing to offer. Next, you have to consider what type of person can do the networking. Obviously, the major qualification is that the individual know Steinfeld. A second critical qualification is that the person be willing to make the introduction, or be flexible enough to be talked into doing so. Begin by making a list of all those you or Trinh know who work with Steinfeld. Add names of those associated with Steinfeld whom you don't know personally. Where do you get this information? You could call Steinfeld's firm and ask the bookkeeper or accountant who the suppliers are. You could have a friendly chat with the secretary or receptionist and get some names. You could talk to others in the business and see whether they know whom Steinfeld works with. In short, get as many names as possible. *Note:* The people on the list don't necessarily have to be salespersons. Unless Trinh has specified otherwise for some reason, the person making the introduction could be a personal friend, a doctor, lawyer, tax accountant, barber, whoever. The key is finding someone whom Steinfeld knows and is comfortable around.

Next, look critically at the list. Try to rank the people in order of who would be the most helpful. Someone whom Steinfeld sees every day would probably be more influential with him than someone he sees twice a year. Someone who is in an equal or superior position to Steinfeld, like his attorney, might carry more weight than someone who works for Steinfeld, like his salespeople. Don't underestimate personal affection. A friend's friends get much more attention than a business contact's friends.

Once you have them ranked according to desirability, rank the names a second time according to feasibility. Whom do you have the best chance of talking into helping Trinh? Who would laugh at your suggestion and leave you feeling rude for having asked? Who would be most susceptible to flattery or to favor-swapping?

Match the lists. If someone is at the top of both lists, that's the person to contact first. Don't ask someone at the bottom of both lists until you are truly desperate.

Finally, you are ready to begin. Decide on the approach (Telephone call? Letter? Personal conversation?) and begin. Work your way down the list. If you have enough names, the law of averages will take over. Someone will be willing to help Trinh.

But what if, despite all your efforts, you fail? You cannot find anyone who knows Steinfeld that is willing to help. Do you quit? Do you want to see Trinh moping around your office for the next month?

You have to regroup. If you can't break through the first line, head for the second one. Instead of trying to get help from a friend of Steinfeld's, try to get help from a friend of a friend of Steinfeld's. A person who will not do you the favor of introducing Trinh to Steinfeld ("He seems like a nice guy, but I've never met him; no reason I should go out of my way to do him a favor") will make the extra effort for a friend. Go through the list process again. Since you already know Steinfeld's associates, make a list of the friends of those associates. Does Steinfeld's banker play golf with the pro at the club? Talk to the pro. Does Steinfeld's wife have her car serviced at the same gas station you do? Talk to the mechanic.

The key is to keep widening your circles. It may take the friend of a friend of a friend before you connect, but at least you *will* connect.

IN RETROSPECT

If you have to choose between two job applicants, each with the same degrees and wanting the same salary, but one has experience in the field and one doesn't, which would you select? Almost certainly, you would select the one with experience. Why? Time-honored experience is a good teacher. We all learn from the past, from our successes and our failures. Networking exemplifies this truism.

Keep track of what you do. Both of us have a large notebook labeled *Networking* which we use daily. Each page in it is headed with a specific problem we used networking to help solve. We list the steps given earlier in this chapter to help specify the problem. We list the qualifications of the person who could help. We list and rank the names of those who could and would be willing to help us. We write down next to each name the day and date and time we contacted that person. If we wrote a letter, we note that a copy of the letter is in our files. If we called, we note that a phone log is in our files (featuring a brief description of the conversation and the outcome). In effect, we have a synopsis of what we said and did, and what the individual said and did. We also note the attitude of the individual. (More is discussed on how to keep an acceptance/rejection log in Chapter 5 on communication.)

Now, this might seem like a lot of paperwork. As a busy businessperson, you may be reading this and saying, "Wait a minute, networking is supposed to make my life easier, not complicate it with a great deal of additional pencil pushing." It's not that bad, honestly. It takes longer for us to write what you should be entering into the notebook, and for you to read our suggestions, than it does for you to jot down the simple facts. If you keep the networking notebook right at hand, it's just as easy to scribble a comment in it as to write the same on your phone log, or on a sheet of scratch paper. And the few seconds you spend working on the notebook are an investment that can save you time later.

We have found that our notebooks are worth every minute we put into them, because of what we call the *déjà vu* factor. In our experience, many of the same problems crop up over and over again. We may need a list of certain organizations today, and a list of other organizations six months from now. The person who knew how to get one list often knows how to get another. If our computer is making strange sounds and hiccuping during printing, we call the same individual who waved a magic wand over it last time and made everything all right. In short, the notebook is a reference that saves us time and frustration. We don't reinvent the wheel each time we have a difficulty. The book has become so invaluable to us that we have it cross-indexed. We can go right to what we need in a matter of seconds.

Dear Abby and Ann Landers often answer questions by going to the experts. They make no bones about the fact that they don't know something, but they do know whom to ask. Many people write to these women, not feeling that the women themselves could give them answers, but that they will know where to get answers. Imagine how interesting and fascinating these writers' lives must be! They probably know a great deal about many topics, are fascinating conversationalists, and play a wicked game of Trivial Pursuit.

You can be in an analogous position in your firm. If you have a good networking book, others will soon recognize the fact. They will come to you for lists of names. You will be their central clearing house. This situation has several advantages.

1. YOU CAN BE INVOLVED IN MANY FACETS OF YOUR BUSINESS

Here, knowledge is power. The more you know about the workings of your firm, the better employee you are. Those who begin at the bottom and make astounding climbs to the top of a profession often do so after having spent time studying the organization and learning its operations, its power structure, its strengths and weaknesses. These people are in the center of the web. You will be there, too. If someone comes to you and asks, "Can you recommend a good moving company that handles corporate accounts?" you might be one of the first to know your office is considering relocating. If another individual wants to know the name of a good class-action defense attorney, you have a hint that your company may be facing a lawsuit.

2. YOU GARNER FAVORS

You have political savvy. Some people will ask for the use of your networking information, giving vague promises of quid pro quo later. However, most savvy workers come prepared, bearing gifts. For a peek into our notebook, for the use of our lists, we have found ourselves the proud recipients of everything from an invitation to the best restaurant in town to suggestions for stock purchases to introductions to important contacts we might never have met otherwise. People understand that your notebook is a resource and that using it demands payment in kind.

3. YOU GAIN RESPECT

Others will be greatly impressed by the fact that you are in the know, that you can handle any situation with aplomb. This respect can be self-perpetuating. When a promotion comes up, everyone will just assume that you are the front runner for it. Management will catch this assumption, figure there are grounds for it, and act upon it.

4. YOU GAIN CONFIDENCE

Think of how many hours you have wasted panicking! If you have a notebook with all this information, you don't have to fuss and fret. You know that you have information or can get it with a few calls or letters or meetings. The longer you network, the more skilled at it you become.

CONCLUSION

Information is power. To gain that power, you need to have networking skills. The purpose of this chapter was to stress the importance of those skills, and show you how to begin acquiring them. You have learned:

- how to identify the problem (getting the specifics of *what* you want)
- how to identify the characteristics/qualifications of an individual *who* can supply what you need
- how to generate lists of those who *could* help and those who probably would *be willing* to help
- how to match the two lists and develop an *organized approach* to contacting the individuals

- how to *get the word out* that you are looking for certain people
- how to *document* your networking activities and use the information to your advantage in the future as well as in the present.

3
IS YOUR "NET" WORKING?

Karen has been working as a public television executive for several years. Her business demands that she attend a lot of cocktail parties and other social events, and generally be around during fund drives. Karen is aware of the fact that one criterion by which all workers at the station are judged (and promoted, and given pay raises, and so on) is how much money they bring in from their social contacts. Therefore, it is absolutely essential for Karen that she be a highly skilled networker. At first, she was just that. For the first five or so years, Karen had an ever-widening circle of contacts. She was always meeting new people, friends of friends of friends. But lately, Karen has sensed that her networking skills have atrophied. As she puts it, "I've become fat and lazy. I felt pressure to network at first, then slacked off when I thought I had enough contacts. But now, there are rumblings of dissatisfaction from my boss. I think it's time to get back into gear again."

John is the best friend of Karen's brother. He has been teaching English to high school students for fifteen years, ever since he graduated from college with a degree in journalism. He is tired of his job, and eager for a change. He thinks he would like to enter the field of journalism. One day when Karen and John were both at her brother's house, the two talked about their job situations. Karen told John how she was feeling the heat to become more active in a network. John countered with his stories of how he feels a little helpless as he has virtually no network at all and doesn't know where to begin. "I don't know anyone who can answer my question. It would be great if I could just sit down and have a long talk with someone who has been through what I am going through right now. Should I give up the security of teaching for the craziness of journalism? Could I get a job after all these years with no real experience in the field? Won't editors prefer someone just out of school, or someone who has been in the field for a while? Can I make enough money to justify giving up my pension, which would vest in just a few more years? And how would I get a foot in the door even to interview, should I decide I am willing to go for a job in journalism?"

Karen and John are typical of many workers. Karen is happy in her career, but stalled, worried that she is not performing up to her maximum. John is at the other end of the spectrum, doing well at a career but unhappy in it, seeking a change. They both need to specify exactly what they want, and then identify how to get that information or take the first steps. They also need moral support. Most of all, they need to begin. Both realize that they they have been talking and talking and talking and not really going anywhere. All they have now are vague fears about what they don't want and even more vague ideas of what they do want.

Does this sound familiar? Are you in a job that you love, but feel you haven't been giving it your all lately, and want to hone your networking skills? Maybe you are dissatisfied with your position, but are worried about giving up the security for something else. Maybe you are concerned that you are not qualified for anything else. After all, in today's job market, everything is so specialized that unless you are trained for something right out of college, you might as well forget about the job, right? Not necessarily. No one expects a nurse to take a job as a CPA right away, or a schoolteacher suddenly to excel as a stockbroker, but with time, information, and the right contacts, these things can happen. If you don't know right now exactly what you want, or if you have an idea of what you want but don't know where to go to find out more information about it, or whom to contact to get started, you are in the same position as John. You are ready to begin the networking process, too.

WHAT IS NETWORKING?

What is networking? A sociologist would have a ball asking persons of different generations to define it. Someone who is older might define a network the same way Webster's dictionary did until about fifteen years ago: "Network: A fabric or structure of cords or wires that cross at regular intervals and are knotted or secured at the crossings." That noun is still in use today. You may hear of a network of highways crisscrossing a map, or a network of veins crisscrossing one's legs. A young person, a child of the electronic age, would almost certainly define *network* in one of three ways: CBS, ABC, or NBC. Hearing the word would send her scurrying to the TV section to find out what's on the tube tonight.

What about those of us in the business world? On a less individual, more generalized basis, how do we define networking? To most of us, the adults of the '80s, *network* is a verb. To *network*, or *networking*, is a buzzword tossed around a lot at work, at social gatherings, in classes.

Networking is an organized method of making links from the people you know to the people they know, gaining and using an ever-expanding base of contacts. Analogous to the terms "the old boys" network, the "new woman's" network, "the grapevine" and "the buddy system," networking is the personal process of linking up with others to exchange information, advice, contacts and support.

Whew! What a long definition. Let's examine, as the lawyers love to say, each element in more detail. Each concept is important; it takes all of them together to make that net that works.

An Organized Method

Note the word "organized." Networking is not a random activity, floundering around aimlessly; it is organizing your activities towards a realistic, achievable goal.

Karen realizes that her station is very active politically, lobbying for causes, working with politicians. Karen decides that if she went into politics herself in a small way, she would make a whole new network of social and business contacts, and be able to help the station and her own career. She thinks she would like to work behind the scenes, volunteering for campaigns or working part time at a politician's office. Karen talks to her boss, who encourages her efforts. Now fully fired up, Karen thinks about how to break into politics. She reasons that the first thing to do is to talk about her goals. She realizes that she would be accepted eagerly if she simply showed up at headquarters and volunteered, but she wants to be more than a stamp licker and errand runner. She wants to be working with the politicians themselves, not with the office staff. Karen begins her Conversation Campaign. She talks about politics and politicians constantly, asking friends what they feel about this candidate, that platform, this issue. She brings politics into the conversation at every opportunity. Is Karen networking? Yes. She is getting the word out, telling as many people as she can about her desire to go into politics.

After a few months, Karen realized that she was asking the same questions of the same people over and over again. She realized that she could benefit from some outside help, and came to us. We presented her with many of the suggestions you have already read about, and, to our delight and her advantage, she followed them carefully. Her first step was to buy an inexpensive notebook and begin labeling pages. Some she headed by name: *Sheila, Frank, Dr. Robison.* Others she titled by position: *Professors, Friends.* Still other pages were categorized by locale: *Los Angeles, Sacramento, Washington, D.C.* On each page, she listed the names and information she had received from the people. For example, under *Dr. Robison* she wrote, "Head of Poly Sci department; former aide to state senator; will give letter of introduction." Under *Sacramento* she wrote, "Sheila, former campaign aid to State Senator Pearson; see Beau for introduction."

Karen's notebook is her way of getting organized. She puts down everything she hears, all the information she receives. Periodically, she goes through the notebook and follows up on her notes. She writes a letter, jots down a response to a letter, makes a telephone call, crosses off a source who didn't pan out, and keeps track of favors granted. By keeping the notebook, Karen knows whom she has already contacted and doesn't pester the person repeatedly. She also knows who is good for an introduction, and who may give her some advice sometime in the future.

Right now, you may be feeling a little overwhelmed. After all, this is a lot of data you are collecting. How are you supposed to keep it organized? Ah, that's the key to being an efficient and skilled networker. It is one thing to collect data, another to keep it will organized so that it is *useful.* It makes no sense spending time and effort gathering all this wonderful information if you don't *use* it efficiently.

Organization is the foundation of networking. How can you become organized? There are many different ways. The following are a few suggestions. The list is by no means exhaustive. Everyone has her own ideas of how to be organized; ask around. People are flattered to be asked, and you will learn new tips that might be perfect for your own situation.

1. CARDS

Index cards are invaluable to the networker. You can carry them with you, write down names, telephone numbers, addresses, all sorts of information. They are small and portable, easy to put in a pocket or purse. They can be cross-referenced. They can be updated instantly; just pull out the card and make a note when you receive a response to a letter or when someone gives you yet another contact.

2. LOOSELEAF NOTEBOOK

Do as Karen did. Have a notebook with pages headed according to your own needs. Keep in mind as you organize yourself that this is all being done for *you.* There is no right or wrong way of keeping track of your channels. If you find a notebook too cumbersome, you might enjoy the cards. On the other hand, if you are like the White Queen in Alice in Wonderland, who strews things about everywhere she goes, cards might not last ten minutes with you.

3. COMPUTER

Never underestimate the many uses of a computer! Maybe you are skilled enough to write a simple program for yourself, one that you can cross-reference and update as needed, or you can purchase and use a program that does this for you. Perhaps you use your computer merely as a glorified typewriter, entering information but not manipulating it. Whatever your skill level, you can use a computer to keep yourself organized. Of course, a computer is not as portable as cards or a notebook, but you can always get an updated printout.

4. CALENDARS AND TIME LINES

One of the greatest tools of organization is the calendar/time line. On our wall, we have a huge horizontal calendar. Instead of the traditional seven boxes across, four or five boxes down, our time line is one long row of boxes all the way across. It takes up an entire wall of the office, but is worth every centimeter. On it, we write down telephone calls that we made and received, note when we have to make new calls, keep track of our correspondence, and so on. If timing is very important to you (for example, if you have only enough money to live on for a few months and need to find a new job quickly), a calendar will serve as an ever-present reminder of time, as well as an organizer.

5. BUSINESS CARDS

These are the greatest aid to networking ever created. We would sooner leave home without our briefcases, cars, or American Express card than without our business cards! Exchanging a business card can lead to unexpected rewards. Anne keynoted the Meeting Planners International Conference in December, 1987, as a result of sharing business cards in an elevator in Washington, D.C. A simple exchange of cards on an airplane resulted in her being the keynote speaker at R. J.

Archer's (a division of Nabisco, Inc.) customer service and sales conference.

Please do not get the idea that these suggestions are absolutes, that they are the only possible methods you can use to become an organized networker. These are simply a few of the techniques we have found helpful. As you talk with others as part of your networking, ask them what works for them, what steps they take. Keep track of their answers, and use what seems valuable to you personally. Keep an open mind; the next technique you hear might just be the one that simplifies your life greatly.

Organization is the first element of networking. Incorporate our suggestions, the suggestions of your friends and associates, and original ideas of your own, to find a system that works for *you*. Then stick to that system. There is no reason for you to duplicate your work, to waste time going over material you have already seen, to irritate friends and associates by asking them the same questions over and over again.

BONUS! A friend of yours might have done much of the legwork for you already! Perhaps he has a notebook of his own, or she has a card catalog that has names you could use. Down the road, your own system may be in demand. Won't it be pleasant to be able to hand over to a friend a neat, organized notebook with names of contacts indexed and cross-referenced? One friend of ours even took her notebook to a job interview with her. The intrigued interviewer asked her what it was. On being shown the notebook, he was so impressed with our friend's organizational skills he hired her, telling her that attention to detail was a quality his firm greatly prized.

Making Links From the People You Know to the People They Know

The first element of this part of the definition is "the people you know." You know a lot of people. If you are in college or have recently graduated, you've met hundreds of fellow students, dozens of professors. If you are in the workforce, you know a lot of people in your office, and many more who are peripherally associated, like salespeople who call, competitors who snoop around, employment agency counselors. Some of you may not be students or workers, but homemakers or retired people who feel you don't have any contacts. But think about it. You know more people than you realize. Do you go to church? Do you belong to any groups, professional organizations? Are you in athletics? Do you go to the YMCA, to scout meetings with your children, to charity events?

One of the most important steps in networking is analyzing your assets and skills. That is, make a list of all the people you know and the resources you bring to others. Again, an organized approach can help. Divide your life into specific areas or categories, like *Church, Volunteer Activities, Children's School,* and write down the people you know in those categories. We all have diversified lives; the key to recognizing your resources is to identify the various areas of your life. Once you have listed as many categories as possible, write down the people you know in each. John took this step, and found he had more friends, associates, and acquaintances than he realized.

"I used to think," says John, "that I had just a few friends and didn't really have any contacts, or at least not any worthwhile ones. Then I began to keep track of what I did over the course of a few weeks, where I went and whom I spoke with. I wrote down my events in a notebook and made lists of the people at those events. I was amazed at how many people I see or talk to in just a week."

The following is a synopsis of John's list. You can make one of your own, following the same format, adding the events and activities that make up your life.

I. WORK/BUSINESS

- fellow teachers
- administrators
- clerical personnel
- other school personnel (like the custodian who fixed my car, and the gardener who gives me advice on my roses)

- parents of students
- former students, now grown
- teachers at other schools, met through professional organizations.

II. FAMILY/INNER CIRCLE

- relatives
- extended family (in-laws, close friends of the family)
- relatives of my relatives (my brother-in-law's parents and siblings)
- business associates of my relatives (the reporter who did a story on my father-in-law).

III. ATHLETICS

- members of my Saturday morning softball league
- casual acquaintances I see during my jogs
- parents of the Little Leaguers I coach
- old friends from my college baseball team
- women in my wife's aerobics classes
- other season ticket holders I sit by at the stadium.

IV. CLUBS/PROFESSIONAL ORGANIZATION

- members of the Lions
- parents of my nephew's Boy Scout friends
- associates in my professional organizations
- friends in our bridge club
- my wife's associates in her professional associations.

V. FRIENDS

- people I socialize with, go out to dinner with, ask to parties
- friends of friends, those people I only see at the homes of mutual friends, but whom I know pretty well

- telephone buddies, friends I rarely see but talk to frequently
- parents of my children's friends, people I know from school or social activities of my children.

We have developed a small chart you may find helpful to you in listing your friends and acquaintances. Note that several people may not fit neatly into a category: What do you do with someone who is a friend and a business associate? Our suggestion is to list him twice. Doing so helps you see that you can ask for help from that person for either a personal or a professional problem. If you list him just once, you might overlook him in another area.

Get the idea? If you do this, you'll be surprised by the numbers and resources available to you. We have found that a good way to help others get a handle on this is to ask them to spend a week, just one week, with a small notebook. Every day, mark down where you go and whom you see. Even something as casual as going to the bank (you might know the teller by name, or be on a "good morning" basis with an officer) can put you in contact with people who can be sources of information. The first step is knowing whom you know, getting their names down. Then, if you are organized, you can go back to those names when the time comes to seek information. Need to find out about how much a journalist makes? Look at your notebook and find out that your father-in-law was once interviewed for a local paper; he probably can give you the name of the reporter who interviewed him. Want to find someone who can tell you where to live in Washington, D.C.? Your notebook tells you that your softball league buddy's wife's family is from D.C.; her parents still live there.

The second part of this element of the definition of *networking* is "to the people they know." Once you are aware of all the people you know, it's time for you to find out whom they know. Put the word out. Don't be shy. Tell others what you are looking for: information on job openings, pay scales, living conditions. Ask *specifically* whether your contacts know anyone who has that information. Sometimes, you have to be direct, as Karen found out.

Table 3-1. PEOPLE RESOURCES CHART

PROFESSIONAL	SOCIAL-PROFESSIONAL	PERSONAL	FAMILY	OTHER
Employer Fellow employees Business clients	Fellow members of professional organizations (Jaycees, union)	Friends Classmates	Extended family (mother of sister-in-law; second cousin) Friends of family members (spouses associates)	Fellow commuters

"I wanted to learn how a particular politician got his start. I could have looked it up in the bio, I suppose, but I wanted more personal information. I knew that this person had gone to the University of Miami, and thought it might be a good conversation point to talk about school. Therefore, I asked around whether anyone had gone to UM. Everyone said no. A few weeks later, I found out through the grapevine that my colleague Lori's cousin had graduated from there. When I asked her why she hadn't told me that, she just looked at me and said, "You never asked me whether I knew anyone who had gone to Miami. You only asked whether I had gone there. I didn't know what you wanted; I thought maybe you were just making a survey."

Karen learned the hard way that some people are very literal. They answer the exact question you ask them, nothing more. Others are busy with their own lives. Although they probably will be happy to help you, it may not dawn on them how much they know. You have to nudge their memories. Instead of a simple yes or no question, like, "Did you attend the University of Miami," go into more detail. "I want to find out some background about the University of Miami to give me something to talk about with Councilman O'Hara. Do you know anyone who went there, maybe in the early '70s?" A question like that would have gotten Karen the name of her friend's cousin, and perhaps more information as well. Note that the question has two parts, the university and the councilman. You might receive an unexpected bonus, in information about the councilman. Just because you are looking for one specific piece of information is no reason not to remain receptive to other information as well.

You may think that once you get the name of an individual, your job is half done. Not so. You still have to contact and build a relationship with that person, still have to try to get information from him or her. Some people are so busy that they resent having the third cousin twice removed of a former neighbors' sister's ex-fiance's best friend's mother contact them from out of the blue and ask a favor. If you want something done for you (say you want the person to go to the housing office and pick up a paper to send to you) as opposed to just answering a few questions, it is imperative that you approach the person correctly.

John: "I was elated when I found out that a friend had a friend who had a friend who used to work for a man who had a sister who is married to a man who is a reporter. I got the reporter's name and telephoned him. It took me about fifteen minutes just to establish who I was, and how I got his name and number. By that time, the man was so frustrated and irritated at my taking his time, that he was in no mood to answer any questions for me. Not only did I lose a potentially valuable source of information, I probably got a few friends in trouble down the line. The reporter was so annoyed that I am certain he called up the others whom I had mentioned as having given me his name and read them the riot act. I feel badly, not just for myself but for them, and for the next poor guy who tries to get information out of the reporter."

John made, and acknowledged, a mistake in going in cold. Imagine how you would feel in the middle of a busy day if suddenly you got a telephone call from someone you had never heard of, someone who is being chipper and ingratiating (as we all are, very self-consciously, when we want a favor) and asking you all sorts of questions. You probably would resent the demands on your time, wonder who on earth this person is, and not feel much in a mood to give any help.

How can you make those links more easily and smoothly? Try the following:

1. ESTABLISH THE RELATIONSHIP CLEARLY IN YOUR MIND

There is absolutely nothing wrong with using a contact who came to you through a veritable maze of connections. Although we all joke about "the third cousin twice removed's ex-wife," sometimes it takes all those people to find a source. Be certain to understand the maze completely yourself before you try to explain it to someone else. It might be easier *not* to go into great detail, but only to give the two ends of the chain. For example, you could say, "I have a friend who knows your friend Susan." *Finis.* If the person with whom you are speaking truly wants to know who your friend is, he or she will ask you. Most often, the person will simply say, "Oh, any friend of Susan is a friend of mine, how may I help you?" After all, we are flattered to be asked a favor, happy to do something for a friend. So keep it simple. Understand the links yourself, but don't go into detail unless you are asked to do so.

2. HAVE YOUR CONNECTION MAKE THE FIRST MOVE

If at all possible, ask your friend or associate who gave you the contact's name, to telephone or write to that person. If your friend Susan can drop a line to her friend Linda saying that you will be telephoning, you have an advantage. Linda has heard of you, seen your name, knows to expect your call. You both save time, not going through the "we have a mutual friend" routine. The contact will be much more receptive to your call.

3. WRITE AHEAD

If your friend is too far removed to make the first move (she only got the name from a friend of a friend of a friend herself, and doesn't know the individual well enough to telephone) or simply doesn't want to take the time to do so, do your own preparation. Unless time is very short, send a letter.

Karen had been told that the politician with whom she was interested in working rarely had time to take his calls, but made a point of reading all his mail. Therefore, she decided to write a letter. She was spared the frustrating phone conversation that John had with his reporter contact. However, she had problems of her own.

"I thought I was pretty clever. I sat down and wrote a letter, establishing who I was, and asking my questions. I was very disappointed when I didn't get a reply. After a few weeks, I was complaining to my girlfriend about the rudeness of the person who didn't even deign to answer my letter. My girlfriend asked to read the letter and said she didn't blame the man; she herself would have had my carefully crafted epistle grace the nearest trash can."

Karen's first attempt was a poor one. Example 3-1 is the letter she sent. See how many weak points you can find, how many places you find she could have improved.

Maybe you've seen a letter of this type. Though Karen made no spelling, punctuation, or grammar errors in it, the letter did not reflect well on her. Let's examine the mistakes she made.

1. *I, I, I*

Karen used the first person pronoun to excess. Although it is logical to use *I* somewhat, she overdid it. The entire letter seemed egotistic. Why not involve the other person? Grammar teachers may not be as strict these days as they used to be in their injunctions against starting many sentences with *I,* but common sense says that varying the sentence form makes the letter more readable and interesting.

2. *GET TO THE POINT*

The reader is a busy person. He wants to know exactly why the letter is being written. What does the writer want from him? By starting off with a biography of herself, Karen wastes the

Karen Warren
1953 Hoosier Avenue
Indianapolis, IN 46219
June 17, 1989

Mr. Mike Vogt
1971 Central Lane
Washington, DC 20817

Dear Mr. Vogt:

I am an executive with KPBS, the local public broadcasting station. I have been working there since 1976, when I graduated from college with a degree in marketing. As our station is very involved with politics, I want to enter politics myself. My friend Mary Lou Burns said that you might be looking for part-time help, as a staff member.

I am not quite certain how you could use me, but I am good in public relations. I work full time, but could probably get some time off to help, if it were a campaign or something pressing. My station is behind me on this.

Please let me know whether you are interested in my services. I look forward to your prompt reply, as I am eager to begin. Thank you very much for all your help.

Sincerely,

Karen Warren

EXAMPLE 3-1

reader's time. She should say right up front why she is writing, what she would like. Then, if she wants, she can add a little bit about herself. Depending on the letter and the situation, background information can be essential (if you are asking someone what he thinks about your chances of getting a job or an interview, of course you have to detail your qualifications; otherwise, he would have nothing to base his opinion on) or irrelevant (if you want to know where the best place to live is, the reader does not need to know that you graduated Cum Laude). Also, in this case the introductory material is confusing. What does Public Broadcasting have to do with politics? Why does Karen want to get into politics, for what specific reasons? The connection is not clear.

3. DON'T SHARE YOUR PROBLEMS

This letter reads as if Karen is dithering. It is not clear whether Karen is going to run for political office herself, or wants to work behind the scenes. And did she really have to come right out and say she doesn't know how she would fit into the reader's office? True as that may be, she could have phrased it a little better. She could write something like, "Your office might be able to benefit from my public relations skills, honed after many years of fund raising for the television station." Note how she is giving the same information, but targeting it more directly. She is making it you-directed ("This is the benefit to *you*") rather than me-directed ("I don't know what to do with myself"). Any politician is going to pick up on and appreciate the reference to fund raising, as well.

Karen might also have given more particulars about her career. She might feel that she is bestowing a favor by offering to become involved with the reader, but he reads the letter as if he is being asked for a favor. By stressing her position and experience, she comes across as a seasoned professional, deserving of respect. Make the reader respect you and think that you are someone who might someday be able to do him a favor in return and the battle is half won.

4. BE SPECIFIC IN YOUR REQUEST

Karen made an incredibly general request: everything and anything that could help. She should be more specific, saying exactly what she would like. Does she want an appointment to meet with the reader? Would she like a letter or a phone call? Would she settle for coming into his office and meeting with his administrative aide? If the reader is not interested in Karen's services, does Karen want him to recommend another politician who might be? There's no sense being shy at this point. Although Karen does not want to sound demanding, she should be willing to make a specific request. If the request is too much trouble, the reader will simply say *no*.

5. DON'T PRESSURE THE READER

Karen made her closing sound as if the reader had to run right out and do her a favor, putting his obviously less important work aside in favor of hers. While it might be a cliche to say, "At your convenience, would you please . . ." good manners do smooth life. The reader recognizes that the writer wants action as soon as possible; that really goes without saying. If there honestly is a deadline, specify it. For example, if Karen is going to be out of the country for a month and wants a meeting before she leaves, she should say so.

6. FOLLOW UP—NURTURE YOUR NETWORK

This letter was—unintentionally, but definitely—rude and arrogant. It put the entire burden of action on the reader. How much more pleasant it would have been for Karen to have written that she would follow up. Perhaps she could have said that she would telephone Mr. Vogt on such and such a day and would be grateful if he could speak to her then. In some way, Karen should have taken the burden on herself, rather than shifting it to a man who she hopes will do her a favor.

Karen was fortunate enough to speak with a friend who gave an honest appraisal of the letter, along with suggestions for revisions. The next letter that Karen sent to another prospective source of information was an improvement (see Example 3-2).

Can you recognize the difference? The second letter was clear, concise, and specific. It was humble without being unctuous, intelligent without being arrogant. Karen did telephone Ms. Gibson at the appointed time. Ms. Gibson had left notice that Karen's call was to be put through, and the two had a conversation. The upshot is that Karen found out Ms. Gibson could not use her services, but she was referred to someone who could. Karen already made a new political contact, Ms. Gibson, who has impressed with Karen's professionalism and glad to help. And now there is the possibility of expanding her network with the new referral.

Gaining and Using an Ever Expanding Base of Contacts

Effective networks must be created and cultivated and followed up. They don't simply happen; you can't purchase, beg, steal, or borrow one. You have to establish one yourself, then care for it continuously and consistently like tending a garden. We have already talked somewhat about establishing one, via the first step, determining whom you know. Let's go into more detail about how to fit those people into a network that is both efficient (one that gets things done right) and effective (one that gets the *right* things done).

There are two types of supporters in a network: maintainers and propellers. Maintainers are those who help you get your job done competently and effectively. Propellers push you into new areas to promote your advancement. Since both Karen and John are seeking to enter new areas, they are concentrating on propellers. Once they have new positions,

Karen Warren
1953 Hoosier Avenue
Indianapolis, IN 46219
June 30, 1989

Ms. Pam Gibson
607 Red Lane
Washington, DC 20817

Dear Ms. Gibson:

Your name came up in a conversation yesterday. Your former employee, Mary Lou Burns, told me how she worked on your reelection campaign three years ago and that you are always looking for new workers to help in your office. I am writing to seek an appointment to discuss how I am help you with your next campaign.

Currently, I am an executive at the public broadcasting station. I have many business and social contacts that might be of use to you. In return, I am eager to widen my own network to include political contacts. I feel we could help each other.

May I telephone you to discuss these matters? Any time you could give me would be appreciated. I will call your office on Wednesday, June 24, at 10:00 a.m. If you cannot speak with me at that time, perhaps you would leave a message telling me when to call again.

Thank you for your help and support. I look forward to speaking with you next Wednesday or at a time after that at your convenience.

Sincerely,

Karen Warren

EXAMPLE 3-2

they don't stop networking, figuring they can sit back and relax. They will simply shift their focus from propellers to maintainers.

HOW ABOUT YOU?

Where are you? Are you reading this book to learn how to use a network to get a new job, or to learn how a network can improve your performance and options in your current job? In either case, it is important for you to identify your maintainers and your propellers. Go through the following exercise, listing the names of your friends and associates who fit the categories. Don't be surprised if several names show up more than once. In fact, you can learn a lesson from that. If you see one individual's name several times in these lists, you know she is an integral part of your professional life and should be cultivated especially carefully.

MAINTAINERS

KEYSTONES

These people form the core of your network and are fundamental to getting your job done (e.g. a secretary or administrative assistant).

_____

_____

_____

EXPERTS

These people do not propel your career; they are peo-

_____

_____

ple in your field whom you
respect and value as professional contacts and who you
would recommend to others.
You would stake your reputation on the professional com-
petence of these people.

TANGENTIAL HELPERS

These people are in related
fields who help you get your
job done (e.g. editor, publisher, and a graphic designer
for a writer).

PROPELLERS

MENTORS

These people guide your career, provide opportunity and
access and teach you the
ropes.

ROLE MODELS

The professional behavior of
these people stimulates ideas
for your future. They have
achieved what you aspire to;
they are examples to be emu-
lated.

HUBS

These people refer you to additional sources of information and people. They suggest helpful connections.

_____

_____

_____

CHALLENGERS

These people cause you to look at your own direction. They force you to face some important questions about your own life.

_____

_____

_____

**PROMOTERS/
RECOMMENDERS**

These people advise you of opportunities and encourage your visibility.

_____

_____

All done? Good. You probably ran out of space, having more names than you thought you would. Since you already made a list earlier in this chapter of all the people you know in all facets of your life, their names were fresh in your mind. What you have done now is classify and categorize them, giving a little more direction to the information.

This may be thought of as your existing network. The names there, if they fit the descriptions, are people whom you already know, people with whom you work and play.

USEFULNESS OF THE NETWORK

It is important to stop and evaluate the usefulness of your network to you. You want to analyze its strengths and weaknesses, learn what parts work and what ones don't. Doing this requires that you understand what you want from your network; what your goals are. You undoubtedly have many goals, personal and professional. For the purpose of this exercise, select just a few, one for each time category. Fill in the following:

My goal in the next six months is: _____

_____

_____

My goal in the next year is: _____

_____

_____

My goal in the next five years is: _____

_____

_____

The most important kinds of support I need now are: _____

_____

_____

Having trouble? Maybe looking at how John filled his out will help.

John is burned out on his career, but is not considering changing right away. He has to finish out the school year, and may even stay one more year. What he wants now is information, something he can mull over. Therefore, he filled out his goals as follows:

My goals in the next six months are: To obtain information about the job market for reporters, to find out the pay scales, benefits, openings and responsibilities. I want to learn as much as I can about what a reporter does, what he is paid, and whether there are many openings in the field.

My goal for the next year is: To talk to several reporters who are on the job now, some who are long-term veterans, some who recently quit other jobs and began reporting. I want to get their personal views of the job. I'd like to talk to reporters in different fields, like editorial writers, political reporters, world affairs reporters, medical beat writers, and so forth.

My goal in the next five years is: To quit teaching and become a reporter. I want to be working for a large newspaper in a major city, preferably doing field reporting.

The most important kinds of support I need now are: Information and contacts. I need to get first-hand commentary, not just facts and statistics from books. I want to concentrate now on learning about the openings, then on getting enough contacts to get an interview to try to get a job.

It was obvious that John put a lot of thought into this. Let's go through it point by point.

1. SIX MONTH GOALS

John isn't ready to put his resignation on the principal's desk, don a pith helmet, and go report from Nicaragua tomorrow. He only wants information. For the next half year, he needs help gaining information, getting the most up to date and honest (not inflated) statistics and facts about salaries and openings.

2. ONE YEAR GOALS

John wants to talk to reporters, to get the real stories from both veterans and novices. He figures that after he has gotten a lot of information on his own, he will be able to have a more intelligent conversation with reporters than he could right now. He is doing his own groundwork, his own research. Once he knows about salaries and openings, he will be able to ask reporters specific questions.

3. FIVE YEAR GOALS

In five years, John wants to be a reporter. He hasn't really decided what type of journalist he wants to be, although he is leaning towards field reporting.

4. KINDS OF SUPPORT

John incorporates his six-month, one-year, and five-year goals in this answer. He needs information now and contacts in the near future.

John did a good job on this exercise, don't you think? You can do the same. Remember: None of this is chiseled in stone. One of the characteristics of a network is that it is changing, flexible, being updated, constantly.

A network is ever expanding. Sometimes, a network can grow and become unmanageable. You may want to divide your network into different levels. There are those people who can provide you information right now, and with whom you should be in daily contact. For example, a boss who knows people whom you want to meet could be reminded (not nagged!) frequently that you are still interested in her help. Other people you can see or speak with or write only once a week or once a month. Keep in touch, you never know when that friendship can be used professionally.

Don't let your network become unmanageable—periodically weed your garden. If you find yourself swamped by having to make calls, write letters, have lunch just to keep in touch, you have let the network control your life. You use it; don't let it use you. Your needs, priorities, and values change. What is suitable and important at one time in your life may be obsolete at another. Be aware of the changes and of your current goals and adapt your network accordingly.

Keep in mind the differences between weeding out and tossing out. It's an excellent idea to keep a professional address book and delete the names of those people with whom you have not had contact for a while and with whom you don't anticipate corresponding with in the near future. But for heaven's sake—let's make that for *your* sake—don't throw those names away. Put them in a file some place. You never know when they will be valuable again.

The same goes for business cards. We all have dozens, even hundreds of cards forced on us at meetings and other functions. As soon as possible after receiving the card, turn it over and use the back for notes. Write down your reactions. How did the person strike you? What did you talk about? Did you have mutual friends, common interests? Keep a current card catalog; put the other cards safely away in another file cabinet. Someday you may get a message on your telephone log, "Elaine Harris called; please return her call." If you can go to your old card catalog, find her card, and read on the back, "Smith graduate, advertising copywriter, son at West Point," think how impressive you will sound when you call her back. Instead of merely saying, "It's good to hear from you; how are you?" You can say, "I always enjoy hearing from a Smith graduate. How's that West Point son of yours?" Won't she be flattered at your remembering all that. The conversation will start off on a more warm and favorable basis, all because you kept a small part of your network intact. You learned to personalize the networking process.

CONCLUSION AND REVIEW

So far, we have been answering the question, *What is net-working?* The answer, discussed in detail, is **networking is an organized method of making links from the people you know to the people they know, gaining and nurturing an ever expanding base of contacts.**

- You now have identified all the many different people you know (more than you realize) by making lists and/or keeping track of your activities for a week or so.
- You know how to stimulate the memories of your friends and associates, to get them to recall people they know who might be able to help you.
- You are able to create an intelligent, professional, soliciting but not demanding, letter to send to someone who might be able to help you.
- You have identified maintainers and propellers in your existing network.
- And finally, you are aware of how to keep your network current and vibrant without throwing away potentially valuable (but presently unused or unneeded) information.

We ourselves use these techniques every day in our professional lives. We recommend their use to our clients and enjoy seeing the results. Again, let us stress that the key to networking is *organization.* For your net to be working, you need to build a strong one, then keep it well maintained. The skills you have learned in this chapter can help you do just that.

4

QUID PRO QUO
(OR, HOW
USEFUL ARE
YOU TO
SOMEONE
ELSE?)

*C*opernicus was not very popular when he hypothesized that the Earth was not the center of the universe, that the planets and the sun did not revolve around it.

DOES THE SUN REVOLVE AROUND THE EARTH?

It is natural for us all to place ourselves in the center of things, to believe that everything revolves around us. A small child is used to being the center of her world. As we grow older, we are forced to recognize that we are just part of a larger picture. Or Quid Pro Quo: when you are part of another's network.

It is especially important in networking to remember that you are part of someone else's network. You cannot simply keep track of your network, blithely using friends and associates and never expecting or dreaming that they someday would want to ask for your assistance. You can gauge how common reciprocity is by the number of clichés our language has expressing the same thought:

- What goes around comes around
- You scratch my back, I'll scratch yours
- Law of cause and effect
- Quid Pro Quo
- You get what you give

WHOSE NETWORK INCLUDES YOU?

You have probably spent a lot of time thinking about whom to include in your network, pondering which friends and associates can do something for you. Let's turn that around. Whom can you assist? Like most of us, you have probably never given much thought to how much you can help others, how much you have to offer. Until and unless we are asked to do something, we usually don't think about helping. However, networks are not one way. Even if the person you help can't possibly seem to be of any assistance to you, somewhere down the line your aid is going to be returned.

EXERCISE: HOW CAN I HELP?

One way to think how you can help others, or "give back" as our author and professional speaker friend Joe Batten says, is to list various people you know whom you can help. For convenience, divide the list into various areas, such as professional/business (you can let an associate address a meeting and get her ideas known, rather than speaking yourself), academic (you could give a speech to a student's or associate's class, or provide materials from your firm for the class to study), personal (you could give a letter of recommendation). *Hint:* To get started, think of all the times you have asked others to help you, to do favors for you. Catagorize those favors.

The following is intended to be a guideline. These are people whom you may be able to help, people who consider you part of their network.

PROFESSIONAL/BUSINESS

- boss
- sales representative
- managers
- public relations staff
- clerical staff
- maintenance staff
- professional organization colleagues
- secretary
- photographers
- printers
- other speakers in NSA who have assisted us

ACADEMIC

- authors
- teachers/professors
- friends or associates who have children in school
- friends in school themselves
- group discussion leaders
- community class instructors

PERSONAL

- hair dresser
- personal shopper
- leisure/sports acqaintances
- hobbyists
- friends
- neighbors
- fellow churchgoers
- book store clerk

> *EXAMPLE:* Shane, who works in a factory, decided to make a list of all the people whom he could help. In his line of work, he never thought of himself as having skills that others would want. However, as he made the following list, he realized how much he could aid his friends and associates, and be a part of their networks.

PROFESSIONAL

BOSS: Go beyond job to write letter to his boss about what a good job he is doing; motivate others to go to meetings when boss is speaking.
COWORKERS: Switch off shifts with friends; give rides; mentor a new coworker.

ACADEMIC

TEACHERS: Give speech on factory work to high school vocational education courses; volunteer as aide in lab.
STUDENTS: Work with students who are having difficulty in school, but who can work well with their hands.

PERSONAL

FRIENDS: Do errands for friends who work "normal" hours instead of my evening shift and who have trouble getting to stores; get part time or summer jobs for friends' kids.

As you read this example, did you think, "That's really very general. Everyone can do those types of things; that's not really networking." Well, yes, it was a general exercise, but also *yes*, that *is* networking. Part of networking is realizing what you can do for others. John Kennedy was being patriotic when he gave his "Ask not what your country can do for you; ask what you can do for your country" speech, but the idea makes a lot of sense in many contexts, not just a national one.

ADVANTAGES OF BEING PART OF SOMEONE ELSE'S NETWORK

It's a fact of life that you will be part of other networks, like it or not. Let's consider the advantages—and later the responsibilities—of being part of a network. Go through the following list; add more of your own if you can.

1. YOU LEARN MORE ABOUT YOURSELF

Suppose that someone asks you to give a speech to her daughter's high school class. While flattered, you might also be scared, worried that you are not a good public speaker, convinced that a crowd of hypercritical teenagers would not respond well to you. Yet, you prepare for the speech, give it, and are a rousing success. You have learned that you can speak well, that you can overcome your fear, that you can hold the attention of even the most critical audience. Maybe next time you will volunteer to give such a speech! Maybe you will start taking speaking assignments at work or talking more during meetings, now that you know what a skilled orator you can be! By having been part of someone else's network, by having learned about yourself, you increase your confidence.

2. YOU FEEL GOOD ABOUT YOURSELF

At Christmas time, as your small children demolish the carefully and lovingly wrapped packages under the tree, you turn to your spouse and smile, truly enjoying the spectacle (the charge card bills won't come in until next year, after all!) and realizing the truth of the maxim, "It is better to give than to receive." The maxim is just as true in the business world of networking. When you do a favor, small or large, for a friend or associate, you are proud of yourself and your confidence increases. Chances are, you go home and casually slip what you have done into conversation, waiting for yet more congratulations, or at least a "That was really very nice of you to do." When you network, you are left with the feeling that you have done something good, something beyond the call of duty (it is not part of your job description to do favors for associates); you simply feel good about yourself.

3. YOU BUILD A RESERVOIR OF FAVORS DUE

You may not have even given a thought to the fact that by doing someone else a favor, that person owes you one in return. On the other hand, you may do the favor in full knowledge that she will someday do you a favor in return.

Ashley: "Two years ago, my college roommate dated Peter, whose parents were deaf. I have several deaf friends and can sign pretty well. When Peter's parents came to school to visit their son and Sharon, I joined the party to help sign. When Peter and Sharon were busy, I took Mr. and Mrs. Mosher around the city, playing their tour guide. I had to take time out of my studies to do so and it was a little bit of an imposition. I forgot all about it until this year. Now I am considering making a job switch and might end up in Washington, D.C. I would like to get some information about housing in that city. I remembered that Peter's parents live in Silver Spring, Md., a suburb of D.C. I wrote to them, asking for information about rentals and costs. They went out of their way to help. Not only did they send me a very nice letter, they went to the apartment association and got brochures, they clipped apartment ads from the paper, they asked their friends for information. I got all sorts of pamphlets from them, and a handwritten list of their recommendations. They even volunteered to go to the specific apartment complexes, once I narrowed them to a few, and look at them for me. I guess my being helpful to a roommate's boyfriend's parents a few years ago is really going to help!"

Ashley didn't help Mr. and Mrs. Mosher because she thought they would help her. She did so because her roommate asked her to. We are always doing favors for friends. How graciously do you respond when someone asks for help? And, just as importantly, do you keep track of the people whom you help? It may seem calculating, but it's a good idea to keep track of the people for whom you do favors. Because Ashley knew that she had done a favor for the Moshers, she felt no hesitation about asking them for help later. She had been part of their network; now she was making them part of hers.

4. YOU BUILD A REPUTATION

Suppose a coworker comes to you, needing your help. If you give that help, and do so willingly and professionally, the word will get around. Soon, others will be asking for your help too. Rather than thinking what a pain all of this do-gooder reputation is, look at it another way. The more favors you do your coworkers, the more you learn. For example, an associate may ask you to sit in on a meeting for her, because she just can't make it. That's an opportunity for you to learn something you otherwise would not have.

In addition to learning, you get a chance to shine. It is much easier to impress a boss when you are speaking at a meeting than when you are merely sitting at your desk, plodding away at routine work. If you can be certain your boss knows you are attending the meeting as a favor to a coworker, adding to your own busy schedule, you will impress the boss as a company player, a person willing to go beyond the job description to doing what needs to be done. And that's a very good reputation to have.

5. YOU BECOME INDISPENSIBLE

Let's face it: There's very little job security these days. Even the big firms that used to hire people for life now have large-scale layoffs. Small businesses are even more prone to layoffs. If someone must be let go, whom do you think it will be: the conscientious worker who does her job, or the conscientious and *indispensible* worker who does her job *and* helps others with theirs? If you are a part of several networks in the office, the word will get around. The people in charge of firing will know that you are simply too valuable to lose.

One of the points in the previous material talked about favors adding up. When you help someone else, you know that person feels a twinge of obligation to help you. Depending on the person, the twinge might be deeply buried or suppressed, but it is there. Your goal, therefore, is to keep track of who has those twinges and how you can best make use of them sometime in the future if you need to.

Think of favors granted as money your bank has available to loan to someone with a good credit rating. That money is not yours yet—you haven't requested it—but your credit is so good, that the loan is virtually automatic. That's great, but only if you know *which* bank has the money for the loan. The same is true of favors. If someone owes you a favor, you can only collect it if you remember the debt. Therefore, it is essential that you be organized in your networking.

KEEPING TRACK OF FAVORS GRANTED

When you get a request for help, be systematic about noting it. Start a card catalog about the solicitor. Write down the person's name, address, telephone number, firm, and position in the firm. Note the date. Describe briefly what you were asked to do. Then, after you have taken the action, specify on the same card exactly what you did and when. If you get a response (perhaps the person will write you a thank you letter or tell you the result of your help), note that as well. Remember learning about the notebook in Chapter 2? If you decide to keep a notebook rather than loose cards, include this information in it. As we said earlier, the more organized you are, the more effective your network is. Keeping everything in one place aids organization. The notebook will have information on members of your network and those people who consider you a member of their networks. Some people send out so many impersonal requests for help and get so many responses that they don't remember someone who helped them. If you want help in the future, it's perfectly acceptable to remind the individual what you did for her.

EXAMPLE: A few years ago John got a request from the brother of a former girlfriend. The man, Jim, asked John to proofread a short manuscript which he was considering sending to a publisher. Jim said that he didn't know anyone else with good grammar skills, and that he would be very grateful if John could help. John wrote the following card:

NAME: JIM GRAY

CONNECTION: Brother of Stephanie Gray. Met in 1974 at Stef's house.

ADDRESS: 22355 Date Palm Drive, Palm Springs, California 92120

TELEPHONE: (619) 555-1212

DATE: Letter received June 20, 1983

REQUEST: Jim wants me to proofread his manuscript, 40 pages. He offers no money, just asks a favor. No connection with his job (he's a CPA in private practice).

ACTION TAKEN: I read the ms, made many corrections on the text, and sent a letter with suggestions (copy attached). I sent it back to Jim (at my expense; no return postage was enclosed) within two weeks.

RESPONSE: I got an immediate thank you note from Jim. A few months later Jim sent me a copy of the magazine that printed his article, along with another thank you note.

John kept a good, complete file. It took him only a few minutes to write down this information. Should he need a favor of Jim in the future, he could remind Jim of this action, giving chapter and verse. See Example 4-1 for a sample letter.

What struck you about the letter? You should have noticed that John kindly, sweetly, but definitely, reminded Jim of their previous connection, of the favor that John did for him. Without making Jim squirm under an intolerable burden, John let him know that there was a debt to be repaid, that it was now Jim's turn to help out.

John's letter was good. Unfortunately, many of us will not write a letter like that on the first try. It takes practice to avoid the pitfalls that can arise in the course of collecting favors owed. There is a natural, human tendency to be shy and hesitant about reminding someone that it is time to pay up (ever wonder how many small, say five or ten dollars loans are never collected between friends because the lender doesn't want to hurt the borrower's feelings?). Sometimes, an unwillingness to collect makes the collector more rude and abrupt than he would otherwise be. In order to avoid these problems, let's first identify them. Example 4-2 is a bad letter that John could have written. After it comes an analysis of the weak points of the letter.

Wow! What a terrible letter! Have you ever received something like this, or—worse yet—sent a curt, abrupt, rude epistle of this sort? Granted, we have exaggerated the weaknesses in this letter to make a better exercise, to make them more obvious in the analysis, but letters of this sort are being sent all around the country right now. Perhaps the following analysis will make you more aware of the defects in the letter, so that you don't reproduce them yourself.

John Althaus
1279 Indiana Avenue
Greenville, IN 46219
July 20, 1989

Jim Gray
22355 Date Palm Drive
Palm Springs, CA 92120

Dear Jim,

How is life in the literary lane? I was thinking of you yesterday, discussing you with several friends who are aspiring writers. I mentioned the manuscript you had me proofread for you back in 1983, and how proud I was to have helped with it, even a little bit. When I saw the article in the magazine, I took vicarious pleasure in it. That was a good, interesting article. Are you still writing?

Speaking of writing, that's what I intend to be doing myself. I have had enough of teaching English for a while, and have decided to become a reporter. I remember your sister telling me once that you were friends with the editor of your college paper. Is he still in journalism, and do you still keep in touch with him? I am looking for reporters or other journalists who can give me information on reporting as a career, who would be willing to answer questions for me. Do you think your friend would speak with me? If so, or if you know others in journalism, I'd consider it a favor if you would give me their names, addresses, or telephone numbers.

I'll be giving you a call next Monday afternoon around 4:00. It would be great if I could get the information from you then. If not, perhaps you could let me know when it would be convenient for us to talk. I'd appreciate any help you could give me. We writers have to stick together!

Yours truly,

John Althaus

EXAMPLE 4-1

John Althaus
1279 Indiana Avenue
Greenville, IN 46219
July 20, 1989

Jim Gray
22355 Date Palm Drive
Palm Springs, CA 92120

Dear Jim,

On June 20, 1983, you asked me to do you a favor. My records show that I did so and returned your manuscript, corrected, on July 3. I was not paid for doing the editing, and I paid the return postage myself.

Now it is your turn to do me a favor. I need to talk to your college roommate, the journalist, or to other journalists you know. Please send me their names, addresses, and telephone numbers as soon as possible.

Thank you for your help.

Yours truly,

John Althaus

EXAMPLE 4-2

1. NO IDENTIFICATION

There was a *six year* span between the time John did the favor and this letter. Probably, Jim has forgotten all about the favor, ("What manuscript?") and all about John. Jim may get the letter and wonder who on earth John Althaus is. In the good letter, John had worked in a reference to Jim's sister, reminding Jim of the connection. In this letter, nowhere is Stephanie mentioned.

2. CURT, ABRUPT, RUDE TONE

In writing, often shorter *is* better—often, but not always. Of course, you realize that the reader is a busy person and don't want to make him spend unnecessary time on your letter. However, there is such a thing as a letter that is too short. This is an example of one. Here, the facts are given—Dragnet style, with no small talk to ease into the situation. Note that in the good letter, there is a pleasantry or two, to set a good mood. Here, the whole tone is stacatto.

3. IMMEDIATE REMINDER OF OBLIGATION

How would you like to get a letter that begins by telling you that you *owe* something to someone? After four years, Jim may have forgotten the debt. While there is nothing wrong with reminding him of it, is there really a need to do so in the first sentence of the letter? Even worse, the reference to records kept is enough to make anyone paranoid! The good letter reminded Jim of the favor he had received without making him feel as if his dossier were on file, taken out and reviewed periodically.

4. REFERENCES TO MONEY

Why not just go ahead and call the guy cheap while you're at it? Why not send him a bill for the postage, and the cost of the time, and interest over the past four years? Nothing like making a person feel small, is there? While Jim should have included return postage (as John noted on his card, which was for his eyes only), not doing so is not worth these recriminations almost half a decade later. The good letter never even mentioned money. The small amount involved and the length of time that has passed, combine to make the topic unnecessary.

5. DEMANDING TONE

This letter *demanded* a favor, rather than requesting one. "It *is* your turn," it reads. How do you suppose Jim is going to react? He just might go ahead and do the favor anyway, acknowledging his responsibility, but more likely, he will toss the ransom note into the wastebasket with the sweepstakes entry forms and forget all about it. Note how the good letter made it sound as if Jim would be doing John a favor on his own, rather than repaying a debt. Both letters got across the "you owe me one" idea, but the good letter let the reader save face and think that the favor was his own idea, done out of the kindness of his heart, rather than out of a sense of responsibility.

6. OBLIGATION FOR ACTION PUT ON JIM

In the good letter, the next step would be taken by John, the favor-requester. John would call Jim at a specific time for the information. In this bad letter, Jim had the burden of action. Jim had to collect the information and get it to John. Making it easy for a person to do a favor greatly increases the chances that the favor will in fact get done. Here, Jim, even while acknowledging that he should do something for John, might just not want to make that little extra effort.

Do you get the idea? Both letters attempt to do the same thing, collect on a favor owed. There is absolutely nothing wrong with doing so. One of the advantages of being part of someone else's network is having a stockpile of favors you can collect on someday. However, the means of collection is all-important.

WHEN TO ACCEPT OR REJECT REQUESTS

As a part of other people's networks, you will get a great many requests for help. Realistically, you may not be able to accommodate all of them. Sometimes, you simply may not want to. However, it is important that you have an organized approach to acceptance and rejection, that you be consistent in your own mind as to what you will and will not do as part of someone else's network.

Criteria for Acceptance/Rejection

1. DO YOU OWE THE PERSON A RECIPROCAL DUTY?

If you have had this person do you a favor in the past, you are duty-bound to help her now. Even if the request is one which ordinarily you would not consider, you should make a little extra effort now because of the debt.

2. IS THE REQUEST REASONABLE?

If the person is asking you to do something illegal or unethical or immoral, you should have no guilt about rejecting the request. If the person is asking you in effect to do his own job, wanting you to take responsibility for something for which he gets paid, feel free to say no. If you are asked in very broad terms to do a rather lengthy project, ask for a more specific set of instructions, or reject the request. However, if you are asked to do something that is within your power and that is relatively well-specified, think twice before saying no. You may need a favor from that person someday.

3. WHAT WILL THE REQUEST COST YOU?

Even a reasonable request will cost you something. You may have to give up your time, or pay something (like the postage in the John/Jim example) yourself. If the amount is small, and you can easily afford to pay it, do so. If the amount is large, don't hesitate to accept with the provision that you be reimbursed.

4. WILL YOU RESENT THE ACTION?

You may be asked to do something which, while reasonable, just plain annoys you. For example, maybe you are asked to go to the airport and pick up a visiting VIP. You just happen to be the only one in the office with a car, the airport isn't far, and you are not working on anything urgent. Obviously, the request is reasonable. However, you don't want to honor it. You don't like driving, you hate driving in the traffic at the airport, you want to· concentrate on your project, and you resent being treated as a chauffeur. If you are going to sulk and stew and let your annoyance ruin your day, reject the request.

5. WHAT WILL BE THE EFFECTS OF YOUR ACCEPTING OR REJECTING THE REQUEST?

For every action, there is an opposite and equal reaction. If you accept the request and do the action, something will occur. Maybe that something will be good: You will be helping a coworker, garnering a favor due, making yourself feel better. Maybe, on the other hand, that something will be bad. You may be wasting your time, being a "pushover" (if you accept each and every request that is made to you, without evaluating it). The same is true of rejecting. If you reject, you might have a momentary tweak of guilt, but save yourself time, effort, and frustration. If you reject, on the other hand, you might alienate a coworker who could be in a position to do you a lot of harm, get a reputation as not being a team player, and sabotage yourself. The moral is, think before you act. Especially if you are being asked to do something relatively significant (like going to a meeting in another city or taking over a whole project from an associate), stop and think about the possible repercussions of both acceptance and rejection.

HOW TO ACCEPT A REQUEST

All right, you have received a memo asking you to prepare a report that really is the duty of a coworker. That coworker has very politely asked you to take over the job, mentioning that you know more about the project than he or she does, that you could get the additional information needed much easier than he or she could, and that he or she is really tied up with another project. You have thought over the request and decided to honor it. Just how do you do so?

Verbal Promises

Sometimes, all the person wants is to hear that you will do something. For example, a coworker might ask you to pass along information you receive on a project. At the time you accept the request, you are not doing anything physical. All you have to do is agree to the request, and the speaker is happy. Even if you never do another thing, never pass along a single document or piece of gossip, you have accepted a request and been a valuable part of someone's network. You have given the requester peace of mind. She knows that she has done as much as she can by asking for help, and is satisfied.

Note: Just because you accept verbally and never take any action does not mean you ignore the favor. Write down on your note card exactly what you were asked, by whom, when, and what you said and did. You can easily bring this into conversation later when you need a favor: "Margie, I learned a lot keeping my ears open about the Opila project for you last month. Sorry there was nothing in your field that I could pass along, nothing you needed. However, how about keeping your ears open for me now on my project? I'd appreciate any scuttlebutt you hear on the bridge contract." Note that the speaker has gently reminded the listener of the favor done in the past, and asked for one herself.

Action

The most common way to accept a request is to do what is requested. Write the report, go to the meeting, doublecheck the letter. But, when you have done the action, *be sure the requester knows you have done the action*. It is common to do something and have no one notice, or to do something and have someone else take credit for it. If you go to the effort of doing the favor for the person, be certain he or she knows about it. You needn't say bluntly, "I did your favor." Something more gentle will work just as well, "Say, I really enjoyed that meeting I attended for you. Glad I could help you out."

HOW TO REJECT A REQUEST

Most of the time, when you receive a request to do a favor for someone who considers you part of her network, you will honor the request. It's not asking too much to have you chat with someone for a few minutes, or to send along information.

Sometimes, you go a step further, go out of your way to do something, like going downtown to the federal building to pick up forms, asking a friend for more information, passing along a request. However, there will inevitably be a time when you don't want to, or cannot, do what you are asked.

Verbal Rejections

Just as there are verbal promises to accept a request from one who considers you part of her network, there are verbal rejections when you say *no* to a request. Most of the time, one simple *no* is sufficient. Of course, you will want to be courteous, kind, and gentle. There are two schools of thought regarding reasons for rejection. Many people follow Disraeli's advice, "Never excuse, never explain." They simply say no, and don't give reasons. Others feel that it is more professional (and allows the requester to save face) to give specific reasons why the request is being rejected.

A friend of ours has a card file she labels "Polite rejections, denials, and refusals." In it, she has a multitude of courteous but definite paragraphs and phrases she uses to reject requests. Whenever she herself has a request rejected, she makes a note of the phraseology and puts it into her file. Some of the phrases are less than courteous or professional, and go in an "Avoid" file. Others are categorized as "Sincere and impersonal," "Humorous," "Promising future action if and when possible," and so forth.

Note: Don't forget to jot down the requests you refused, as well as the ones you accepted, in your record. Suppose that you need a favor down the line. You can go to your card catalogue and see whom you have rejected and not ask those people for favors. Often, there is more than one individual in an office who can do something for you; it's logical to ask the person who has not been turned down by you. You have a much better chance of getting your request accepted.

Action _____

Obviously, taking no action is one way to reject a request. A well-written, courteous request will leave you an obvious out, such as, "If you have an opportunity to do so, please send me material on . . . . " You truly might not have the opportunity to do what the requester asked, or may decide not to do so.

Sometimes, you are asked to refrain from doing something; you reject the request by doing that action. For example, if your coworkers ask you not to send them copies of every memo you write, yet you feel it is important that you do so, you deny their request by continuing the paper flurry.

As with verbal rejections, rejection by action can be done politely or rudely. Most often, it is a good idea to accompany your action (or nonaction) by comment. You could talk to the requester and say why you are not going to do the action or are going to continue doing it. You could send a memo on the topic. Or, if you are feeling somewhat timorous, you could talk to the office gossip, that person who heads the grapevine and makes certain everyone hears everything. Talking to that individual will ensure your message is received and allow you to shirk a face-to-face confrontation.

Some people just won't give up. You may have a coworker who makes the same request of you dozens of times, sometimes intentionally, sometimes unconsciously. Maybe that person really needs the favor, really needs help and feels that you are the only one who can help. Perhaps the individual truly can't understand why you rejected his request and thinks if only he is persistent enough ("The squeaky wheel gets the grease") you will change your mind. How do you handle someone who won't take no for an answer?

1. BE CERTAIN YOUR REJECTION WAS UNDERSTOOD

Sometimes, we try so hard to be polite and solicitous of the other person's feelings that we bend over too far. If you are so courteous that your rejection ends up sounding like an acceptance or a "we'll see," no wonder the other person persists. Think back to what you said; reread what you wrote. Did you *specifically* say no, or did you just hint that you were "not inclined to take that action at this time"? Clearly, the latter response gives the requester hope, and encourages him to repeat his solicitations.

2. DETERMINE THE NEED OF THE REQUESTER

You may have thought that the favor being asked of you was not all that important. If you don't address the meeting, for example, surely someone will. (This is the same approach people have about giving to charity: Someone else will volunteer.) However, if the person feels so strongly about getting your help that he is still importuning you quite some time later, reevaluate the situation. Maybe the requester is desperate and sincerely needs the help that only you can give. Offering that help after all can gain you a great deal of gratitude.

3. REEVALUATE YOUR REASONS FOR REJECTING THE INITIAL REQUEST

Maybe you were just having a bad day when you said no. Maybe the tone of the requester irritated you and made you turn down something you normally would have been happy to do. Maybe you thought the project would entail too much work, but now see that you could do it easily. Make an honest assessment of your reasons for saying no. If they are still valid, stick to your rejection. However, if you are secretly rather ashamed of your churlish behavior in denying the request out of hand, admit it and change. If you didn't give the requester reasons for the rejection in the first place, you don't need to give him reasons for your changing your mind now. However, if you did give him reasons for the rejection, you certainly should explain what has changed in the interim so that he will understand your reasoning and respect you.

4. DON'T CONSIDER CHANGING YOUR MIND A SIGN OF WEAKNESS

You might be thinking that if you give in after all you will be considered a lightweight, a pushover, easy to manipulate. There are times when that could be true. However, part of being a professional is recognizing that situations change, and going with that change. If you change for a good reason, no one will think less of you. After all, even Coke changed its formula after 100 years—then changed it back again!

CHANGING AN ACCEPTANCE TO A REJECTION

Suppose that someone asks you to do a favor. Proud of being part of such an effective network, you immediately agree—too immediately, as it turns out. As you begin to do the favor, you find that it is going to take more time, energy, or even money than you had anticipated. In short, you want to change your acceptance into a rejection. But doing so is a very delicate operation. The following suggestions can help.

1. CLARIFY EXACTLY WHAT DOING THE FAVOR HAS ALREADY COST YOU

Before you tell someone that you are going to stop doing what you have been doing, you want to be certain in your own mind how much time and effort you have already put in. For example, maybe someone, knowing you are a computer whiz, asked you to evaluate the software he is contemplating buying. You already put a dozen hours into doing so. Or maybe someone asked you to find a specific piece of information that required your making long distance calls, costing time and money. Write down *exactly* what the costs were. And don't exaggerate. If they are inflated, the other person will sense the fact and resent it. He will in effect be thinking, "You don't have to lie about this; just tell me you don't want to help me."

One more point: When you write down your expenditure, you may find that it is not as great as you thought. For example, maybe it only seemed like you were on hold for ten minutes when you made that long distance call, but it was actually more like two minutes. You may be chagrined to find that you were overreacting, and can still do the favor after all.

2. ESTIMATE THE EXPECTED ADDITIONAL COSTS

Once you know how much something has already cost you, try to estimate the remaining cost. You might have to put in at least another dozen hours evaluating the software, or make a half dozen additional calls. Write it down. You want to be able to tell the person, "I have to stop this project now, because it has already cost me so much in time and money, and is going to cost me this much more." When you do this, you are more firm in your resolve to quit the project. You alleviate any guilt feelings you may have at being a quitter, since you see the costs. And you show the other person in quantitative, objective terms why you can't go on.

3. SHARE WHAT YOU HAVE ALREADY LEARNED

If the project is important, chances are the other person will find someone else to continue the work. Be generous with what you have already accomplished. Give the information, discuss what you learned. There is no reason for you to be petty and keep the knowledge to yourself. Why should someone else have to repeat your work?

4. SUGGEST A SUBSTITUTE

If you had accepted a task, the other person probably was relieved to leave it to you. He stopped looking for anyone else, naturally, and waited for your help. Now when you reject the project, he suddenly is adrift, with no one else to turn to. You can lessen the negative feelings by suggesting someone else who can help. Give a name and a number. "You know, I think Colleen Thomas would be just the person to help you on this. You can reach her at 555-1212. Be sure to mention my name."

5. APOLOGIZE BUT DON'T GROVEL

You are in the wrong. You accepted a project that you probably shouldn't have accepted, and put the other person in a bind. Say you are sorry. But don't overdo the apologies, almost groveling. Doing so makes you resentful, and causes the other person to inflate the importance of the apology. After all, if you feel *that* badly, you certainly must have done something terrible.

6. MOVE ON

There might be a little embarrassment between the two of you now. You might be hesitant to ask the other person to help you out, seeing as how you just let him down. And he almost certainly is going to be wary of asking you for another favor. So you let these feeling come between you and hurt what should be a strong networking relationship. It is up to you to make the first move. Volunteer to do something else for the other person, if that is feasible. Note that you are not going to go overboard here either. You could call up one day and say, "I heard your company is looking for a new computer operator. Here's the name of someone I think you might like." A small referral or favor can put the two of you back to rights. Forget the acceptance-turned-rejection and move on.

FOLLOWING UP

Earlier we discussed the importance of following up when you are the one requesting a favor. There is no excuse for not thanking the person who does you a favor, or for not sending a polite "thanks anyway" note to someone who denied your request. But what about when you are the one who is having the request made of her?

Follow up is important in this situation, as well. Remember the card catalog that John (in the Jim and John example) kept? That was a type of follow up, noting who wrote him a thank you letter, what action resulted. However, that was follow up of how the other party responded. You also need to follow up on your own.

If the individual asked you to do something that has a definite result, mark a date on your calendar to write or call to find out about the result. For example, if you teach a class as a favor to a friend who has to be out of town one week, call a few weeks later and see how the students did when tested on that portion of the course you taught. If you are asked to create a letter, find out later what comments, what type of response the letter had. By doing so, you help both yourself and the other person.

You help yourself because you learn more about your own performance. You get valuable feedback, information you have to use in the future. You also get a reputation as a person who does follow through, a professional who finishes what she starts, who cares enough to see a project through to the end, even when it wasn't her own project to begin with.

You help the other person as well. He probably hesitated to ask you for a favor, worried about rejection. Even though you accepted, he still might feel uneasy, thinking that your acceptance was grudging. By following up, even when you don't have to, you indicate to the requester that you in fact enjoyed what you had done and want to know what happened. You take some of the burden of guilt off his shoulders. If a house guest of yours broke a glass, wouldn't you immediately try to make him feel better over it, assuring him that it was all right, no problem? That's part of graciousness, of good manners. There's no reason good manners can't be part of the business world as well.

CONCLUSION

Quid pro quo is a reality of networking. You too are part of other people's networks. When you recognize those networks, you can better see the advantages your membership in them brings you. We discussed with you some of the ideas we have found helpful to our clients on how to reject a request (verbally or via non-action), how to reject repeated requests, and how (this might just be the most difficult task) to change an acceptance to a rejection. We hope we got across to you one very important facet of networking that too many busy, harried business people neglect: the follow up. When you grant a favor, follow through and then follow up, just as you would when requesting a favor. Good communication skills can aid in an effective follow up. These skills are discussed in the next chapter.

5
COMMUNICATING WITH EFFECTIVENESS AND POWER

*C*ommunication. What does that term mean to you? Do you consider it a buzzword, a bit of business jargon that has its vogue? Do you, along with many others, get frustrated in communication, finally blurting out, "Oh, you know what I mean!" Ever notice that it is only the poor communicators who have to resort to that defensive posture? The good communicators continually work on their skills, recognizing how important they are.

THERE ARE NO MISTAKES IN COMMUNICATION, THERE ARE ONLY OUTCOMES

You network because you want to get something done. Good communication is directly related to getting things done. After all, if no one knows what you want done, or how to do something the way you'd like, how well are you going to like the outcomes? The better the communication, the greater the productivity. In virtually every business situation, the clarity and precision of communication is a key factor in how well, quickly, and efficiently the job gets done. Consider the following statistics:

- We spend approximately 80% of our waking hours in some form of communication.
- Success in the workplace is 85% dependent on effective communication and interpersonal networking skills.
- Seventy percent of mistakes made in the workplace are attributed to ineffective communication.
- Approximately 75% or more of all messages are communicated nonverbally and relayed in the tone of the voice.

Stop and think for a moment about your own business or organization. Can you recall a time when a less-than-clear direction resulted in a botched-up job, in a missed order, in ill will and bad feelings? When did you last read a memo that left you shaking your head, needing to speak with the memo's writer in order to clarify an important point? Just think of the time and money wasted by unclear communication. You might have had to stop working on an important project, seek out the individual who issued the fuzzy directive, and spend time going over it with him. If the writer created the memo a few days ago, more time will be wasted while he gets his mind back on your problem, trying to recall what he meant. Everyone loses in this situation. The reader is frustrated, irritated by not having clear directions, and secretly feels insecure, wondering whether the fault is hers for not understanding the memo. The writer is annoyed at having to go back and do the job a second time, and probably somewhat embarrassed at his failure to communicate the first time. The company loses the productivity of the workers during this period. This loss of productivity is very real. It's been said if each of the more than 100 million American workers prevented just one $50 error by communicating more effectively, over $5 billion additional profits could be realized by their organizations. The increasing size and complexity associated with most organizations means that the loss could be even higher!

You were asked earlier what communication means to you. While everyone has a different definition, the experts have come up with a standardized one to clarify the process.

THE THREE ELEMENTS OF COMMUNICATION

1. Organize Thoughts
2. Encode Meaning—Decode Meaning
3. Clarify Affirm Message
   a. Feedback
   b. Action

1. ORGANIZE THOUGHTS

To use your network effectively, you have to be clear in what you want. Before you can get your idea across to someone else, you must know yourself what that idea is. Sometimes, we try to skip this step. There is nothing worse than going into an associate's office and stammering and stuttering for five minutes, saying virtually nothing, and leaving with a red face and the knowledge that your associate had no idea why you just wasted his time. Get a clear idea of what you want to communicate *before* you begin the communications process. Think of this step as having a shopping list before you go to the grocery store. If you don't have the list, what happens? You are distracted by everything up and down the aisles, end up purchasing things you didn't really come to get, and over time maybe even put on a few pounds as a result! If you don't have a mental list of what you want to communicate, you will be distracted by all the thoughts scattered throughout your mind, blurt out many of them, and leave your speech "flabby" rather than tight and succinct, as a good professional's should be.

This "flabby" speech can be especially destructive to a networker. You have been reading throughout this book that one of the keys to successful networking is being organized. This is true for speaking, as well as for keeping the notebook. Suppose you want to establish contact with a computer scientist, because you might somewhere down the line be put in charge of establishing a computer training program for your office. You know little about computers, and would not be teaching the course yourself, but would be responsible for finding a firm to offer classes and continuing instruction. Since you know it is only a matter of time before the office is fully computerized, you very wisely think you'll begin establishing a computer contact network now.

You are at a party and are introduced to Alan, a systems software engineer. You smile and say, "Oh, I don't know what that is. My office might be having computers soon, I'm not sure. We may be having classes." On and on you ramble, telling Alan more about your office than he ever wanted to know. Yet, when he finally makes an excuse and drags himself away, you are mentally kicking your bottom for what you forgot to say. You never did get around to asking him whether he, or his firm, does any computer set up and instruction, what the rates are, what his qualifications are, whether he can recommend a course, and so on. You have dozens of questions that come to mind as you watch Alan's back vanish in the distance. All you did was blather about yourself, when you really wanted to get information from him. Had you been organized, maybe given a little thought to specific questions earlier, you could have come up with them even at an unexpected encounter like this one. If worst came to worst and you knew you were not organized, what's wrong with the honest approach? "Alan, our firm might need computer instruction, and I will probably be put in charge of getting it. If you were me, what kinds of questions would you be asking, and what information would you be seeking?" Most people would probably prefer a direct approach like that, to an oblique, time-wasting one. If you are not organized in what you need, at least be organized enough to ask the right overall questions. Let your listener provide the specifics.

2. ENCODE MEANING—DECODE MEANING

Once you know *what* you want to say, you need to determine *how* to say it. This process is called encoding. You determine what words to use—and as you know, the words can make all the difference.

Suppose you are going to tell an employee that her work is adequate, but not brilliant, that you know she can do better if only she tries harder. How would you say that? You could conjure up memories of a third grade teacher who wrote on the report card, "Not working up to her potential" and unctuously say, "Oh, but you can do soooo much better, if only you'd try!" How do you think that makes the listener feel? Probably, she will ignore your communication, thinking it is childish and insincere, the standard speech everyone gets to motivate her to higher performance.

On the other hand, you might communicate the same message with more specific words, and in a different tone. You could say, "Your work is average, but from an above average worker like yourself, that level is surprising. *I* know you are capable of better work; *you* know you are capable of better work. Let's see you make the effort, and prove us both right." Note that you have worked with the same basic idea, but have encoded your communication in a different way. Your listener feels that the message was sent to her personally, was not part of a boss's manual *How To Talk To Your Employees*, and is willing to act on what you say.

The flip side of encoding a message is decoding it. The sender or communicator, encodes the message, deciding what to say. The listener decodes it, determining how she is going to interpret what is said. If you are listening to someone who is sincere this time but usually is hypocritical, no matter how well he encodes his message, you are going to decode it to mean that he is insincere. How likely are you going to be to want to be a part of his network, or to make him a part of yours?

Michael is a hail-fellow-well-met type, always ready with a big smile and firm handshake. He is known for his smile and his promises, which he rarely fulfills. It's common practice for him to toss off a "Let's have lunch, and I'll introduce you to a few prospective clients" every time he sees an associate. Most of his friends and business contacts have learned to take anything Michael says with a grain of salt.

Michael has recently been informed by his boss that he needs to bring more work into the office. The boss suggests that he exchange clients with others, maybe sending some of his accounting clients to his real estate friends in return for referrals from them. Michael has compiled a list of friends and associates who might be able to send work his way, and agrees with his boss that the quid pro quo approach is his best bet. He is going to recommend to his clients that they hire the professional services of others, and then hint to those others that they send their own clients Michael's way.

The first person Michael sees on the day he begins to put this plan into operation is David. "Hey Dave, good to see you. You know, I have just sent some business your way. I told several of my clients what good deals you have in real estate now. These are hot prospects, so treat them right. And you know, I could use a little new business myself, so send 'em along!" David, well accustomed to Michael's bluff, exaggerated ways, smiles, promises to do just that, but of course never does. The problem is not that David is unwilling to help Michael, but that he doesn't take him seriously. Michael has encoded his message the same way he encodes all the others, with overly hearty, apparently insincere overtones. No one is going to take him seriously.

Michael needs to recognize this, and take steps to separate his normal communication from his networking communication. No one is suggesting that the leopard change its spots, simply that there be some indication to the listeners that what is about to follow is serious. Michael might be better off with more facts in his conversation, such as, "David, I need clients. My boss has informed me that I have to pull in more business. I imagine that you have the same situation, being in a personal services business. How about exchanging clients? I will recommend you to my clients who have money to invest, and you can give my card to your clients. We can help each other."

What a difference! First of all, the tone is serious, professional. There is a change in the way the message is introduced. Previously, Michael's technique was to start off by promising the sun, moon, and stars, gratis. He played The Big Man, doling out favors. Now, he intentionally changes his approach to exact opposite. Instead of starting off with what he is going to do for the others, he makes a point of stating that he needs help. Since this is unusual, it is an attention getter. Second, the comment is full of facts, cold hard data, rather than just nebulous promises. Michael tells why this situation is different, gives the specifics of what is going on. He then addresses what he wants, stating exactly how he proposes to get it. It might have been even better had Michael had some names prepared, such as, "Last week, I gave your name to Don Brinkley, Gene Ebert, and Alice Clapton," to show he was serious, but he has made a start. By encoding the message differently, he ensures that it is decoded differently, and taken seriously.

3. CLARIFY/AFFIRM MESSAGE

The final step in communication is making certain you understand what was communicated. Most of us do this every time we repeat a telephone number that we just obtained, or repeat a name we just heard in an introduction. On the telephone, we say, "Let me repeat those directions back to you, to be certain I have them correct." In business, not clarifying a message, not affirming that it was received can have costly consequences.

There are two parts of the clarification/affirmation process. The first is feedback (about which much more will be said later in this chapter). Feedback consists of reacting to the communication, in a positive or negative manner. The second is action, doing something in response to the communication. For most of us in business, the purpose of communication is to stimulate action. We tell our shoppers of a bargain to encourage them to purchase. We tell our clients of changes in the law to have them change their procedures. And in networking, we tell others of our desires in order to get information from them that can help us fulfill those desires. If it is not absolutely clear what those desires are, there can be some ludicrous results.

Jose hopes to have his company pay for continuing education for its employees. He thinks that the best way to get this is to create a groundswell of support for the idea, to have everyone talking about wanting more classes. Jose has a good, strong network, and begins putting the word out. One of the first people he talks with is Peggy. Peggy listens to Jose's speech with enthusiasm, and rushes away to spread the word. In a few weeks, Jose is called into his boss's office and asked how much he will need for the project. When Jose, thinking that the boss means how much will it cost for Jose to take a semester's worth of evening classes, answers "$500.00," his boss raises his eyebrows and comments briefly that that seems like a good deal.

Jose spreads the good news around the office that the firm is going to pay for evening courses for its employees. Everyone is congratulating Jose, who feels like a big man. Unfortunately, the bubble bursts the next morning, when he gets a notice on his desk that "Your services are being contracted to teach the following evening courses to our new employees, for the sum of $500.00 per semester." Jose quickly realizes that his message had gotten garbled.

Instead of hearing that Jose wanted to attend classes (and wanted to extend that privilege to everyone else), management got the idea that Jose wanted to teach classes. There was a major mix-up in communication. Jose eventually traced it back to his colleague Peggy, who freely admitted that she had thought Jose was offering his teaching services at night. When asked how she could think such a thing, Peggy replied, "Well Jose, what did you expect me to think? You corner me and start talking about classes, and don't I think that they are important, and you are trying to get funding for additional instruction. I thought you meant *you* were trying to get funding, that is, to be paid, for offering the instruction. You should have made it clear you wanted to be a student, not a teacher." There was enough blame to go around. Jose was fuzzy in his communication, and Peggy didn't take the time to clarify what she thought she was hearing. Action was stimulated, but the wrong kind. It took time and effort (and embarrassment) to straighten out what could have been prevented in the first place with a little clarification. It may seem trite to say, "Now let me get this straight. What you are saying is . . . ," but it is important. A good networker knows that he is getting his desires and goals across clearly, and that he is understood by his listeners.

COMMUNICATIONS OBSTACLES

Games Playing

There are many hurdles that a good speaker and writer has to get over in the course of communicating. One of these is the games playing that occurs in even the most friendly, informal companies. What is games playing? It is the Tom Sawyer Skill, the ability to persuade others to do something for us, that helps us reach our goals with the willing help of others who feel that they are in fact benefiting themselves.

Alan needs to get a list of all the firm's customers who in the past year have purchased a certain color of paint. He could go through the files himself, looking up names and addresses. Naturally wanting to avoid the tedious process, he turns to the computer programmer. "Say, Cathy," he begins, "I was thinking about you yesterday. I know you are eager to get a promotion, and I think I know of something you can do to catch the boss's eye. Ms. Johnson really likes organization and attention to detail, and is impressed with those who give a little more to the firm of their own initiative. I remember her telling me when I was hired that she likes to see people beginning projects on their own, rather than always waiting for directions and instructions. I was trying to think of something our firm could use that we don't already have, and came up with a cross-referencing program. Why don't you spend a few hours and create a simple program that lets each customer's info be entered then accessed based on a number of different categories? Just think how quickly you can get information when Ms. Johnson requests it, and how impressed she will be by your initiative."

Note the excellent games playing Alan is doing. First, he flatters Cathy by making it seem as if the entire point of his communication was to help her. He begins by telling her that he is thinking of *her*. Obviously, she is going to be much more receptive to what he has to say next than she would be had he said, "I've got a problem" or "I need a favor." Next, Alan shows Cathy how doing the project can benefit her, shows her what's in it for her. By this time, Cathy can't wait to hear what needs to be done. Alan finally tells her the project, almost casually, belittling the time and energy needed to create it. He ends on yet another personal note, reassuring Cathy of the benefits she will reap from her productivity. Nowhere does he mention that his goal in all of this is to get the information for himself.

How often do you suppose Alan will be able to work this ruse? It depends. If his statements are based on fact, if indeed Ms. Johnson does reward initiative and will be impressed by Cathy's extra work, Cathy will be willing to listen to Alan again. However, if Alan takes the information and benefits from it himself when Cathy does not, she will feel fear and anxiety when next he approaches her with an idea to "help" her. This fear and anxiety will make her much less receptive to anything he says. The communication process between the two will be inhibited. Cathy will already have a barrier up, worried that Alan will be making work for her that will only help him.

Interpersonal Dynamics

A second communication obstacle deals with interpersonal dynamics. The relationship between the communicators significantly affects all communications. The following are examples of how the people, rather than the subject of the conversation, affect the communications process.

1. *What the communicator intends to say, or honestly feels she is saying, may not be what she is saying in fact.*

   EXAMPLES: Dayna has been working as an accountant for only a month. Although she is skilled, she has not yet learned all the specialized vocabulary that her tax firm uses. Wanting to be accepted and to impress others, she drafts a memo using jargon she has heard in the office. Unfortunately, she misunderstood the jargon, assigning it a meaning the others had not intended. When the others read her memo, they acted on it according to their interpretation—which was not what Dayna had intended. The work was not acceptable, and had to be redone, at considerable expense.

Marcy is using her network contacts to get the word out that she wants an introduction to a company president who is known for being a recluse. Somehow, the message is garbled, and results in her listeners thinking that Marcy knows the president. Her colleagues clamor for her to introduce them to the reclusive president. Marcy has to spend time and effort setting the record straight. In the process, she hurts the feelings of several colleagues who don't believe her, who think that she in fact is simply refusing them an introduction out of personal spite.

2. *We only hear what we are willing to hear.*

EXAMPLES: Keith had spent a long time on a presentation to an important client. He had charts, graphs, and other artwork, much of which he had done on his own time. He was very impressed with himself, and sure the client would love the work. When Keith's boss looked at the work, he said that while the quality was excellent, the thrust was "way off the mark. Keith," said his boss, "This ad campaign of yours seems geared towards the upper class, high-income market. The manufacturer told us he is selling bottom of the line merchandise, trying to capture a larger share of the low-income market." Keith had been so eager to work out the campaign that had been in his head for the product that he didn't really listen to what the client was saying. Keith had wasted time and energy, lowered his stature in the eyes of his boss (who, rather than being impressed with the work, was dismayed that Keith had so obviously missed the mark completely), and irritated the client who is going to have to wait longer for his campaign. Keith heard what he wanted to hear, rather than what was being said.

James had been told by Cindy that she would be glad to help him whenever she could. James needed some referrals for help when he opened his new law office, and called upon Cindy. She helped him find a legal secretary and office manager, and felt she had done her job. However, James kept calling and calling, making a pest of himself. Finally, Cindy told James, "Glad as I am to have helped you, I think I have put enough time into our career. I have to get back to my own job now." James felt so guilty over using Cindy's time that he began bending over backwards to help her, sending her referrals she didn't ask for, having others offer their help to her. He was now making a pest of himself rather than helping, rather than asking for help. What he had heard Cindy say was, "It's your turn to help me now; I have helped you." what she really was saying was, "I've done my best for you, now leave me alone." James heard what his overly solicitous conscience prompted him to hear, rather than what was actually being said.

3. *A communicator often uses unique words that are misinterpreted by the listener or reader.*

EXAMPLES: Phil prides himself on his wry sense of humor. He often uses words sarcastically, intending the opposite meaning of the term. When he compliments someone on her work, he tells her how "bad" it is. When he wants something done quickly, he informs the worker, "It's due around the turn of the century." Most of Phil's co-workers are accustomed to his opposite vocabulary, and take it into account. However, Susan, Phil's new co-worker, took a memo that said, "Don't bother keeping me informed; just hand me the final calculations" literally. When he hadn't been told of any progress after a week, Phil thought Susan had not done any work on the project, and assigned a second worker.

Eva called on one of her networking contacts. "Shayna, if you ever have a spare minute, nothing major, I would appreciate your sending me a note on the computer system your office uses. I am thinking about switching over, and could use the info. Just a few facts." Shayna took Eva at her word, and sent along the brochures the company had supplied. What Eva really wanted was all the information Shayna had, including the comparison shopping the firm had done, and follow up reports. However, Eva's expressions like "Nothing major" and "Just a few facts" were interpreted literally by Shayna, who did just the bare minimum. Eva felt resentful that she had been slighted, and a good networking relationship cooled, for reasons Shayna never figured out.

4. *The timing and location of the communication affect its interpretation.*

EXAMPLES: Paul and Bill were at a hockey game when Paul leaned over and said, "I've been thinking about the new product we want to introduce. What do you think about increasing the ad budget significantly and making a big splash up front?" Bill, intent on the action of the game, nodded absently. The next week, he was shocked to find a bill for a huge ad campaign on his desk. "How could you have taken me seriously?" he shouted at Paul. "We were at a hockey game; did you really think I was going to make that kind of decision there? I was barely listening to you. You could have asked me to sell you my house for a buck and I would have nodded and agreed!" Paul felt that a social event, especially a sporting event, was a place where business people did in fact discuss business and make deals. Bill, on the other hand, took his sports seriously and had asked Paul along merely for the pleasure of his company, not to conduct business. Because the two men interpreted the importance of the locale and timing differently, there was miscommunication and a definite business difficulty. The net failed, because it was depended on at an inopportune moment.

Joe and Leo were at a sales seminar. The speaker was a very enthusiastic seller who motivated everyone in the room. In the heat of the excitement, Joe leaned over and said to Leo, "Let's get together and join resources. Maybe we could improve our sales by talking over techniques." Leo, who knew Joe only slightly, figured that Joe was simply carried away be the moment, and didn't take the comment seriously. When Joe didn't hear from Leo for weeks, he wrote him out of his networking file, shrugging with the comment, "If he can't follow through on his obligations, who needs him as a resource?"

5. *The interpersonal relationships between the people involved, as well as the overall organizational climate, influence communication.*

EXAMPLES: Alice just transferred from a small, family-held business in which much business was done around the water cooler to a very formal, buttoned-down firm that wanted everything in writing. When Alice casually mentioned to her assistant that she wanted something done, Steve nodded. Alice assumed the project was as good as done; Steve assumed that if Alice were serious, she would draft a memo to him giving him more details. The project wound up getting done weeks late, due to a late start. It took Alice a few weeks to recognize that a casual request in this new firm held no weight, that anything that needed to be done would have have to be put in writing.

Max and Alexandra have been part of each other's network since college days. Two decades into their career, they have done so many favors that both have lost count. When Max mentioned that his niece, an electrical engineer, was looking for a job in Alexandra's city, Alexandra spent a lot of time lining up interviews and getting information. Max had neglected to mention that his niece already had a position with a firm, and was actually just considering making a geographical switch, but remaining with the same firm. The relationship between the two networkers was so strong that one hastened to help before it was clear exactly what was needed. Max had not asked Alexandra for help, but because of the friendship, Alexandra had done work on her own. The obstacle, ironically, was an overzealousness to aid.

Conflict

So far, you have learned about two obstacles to communication; games playing and interpersonal dynamics. There is a third one, one that is perhaps the most common in an organization: Conflict. Whenever there are people working together, there is bound to be some conflict. If this were not so, everyone would be part of one big happy network, only too eager to help one another. The key is recognizing conflict for what it is, then either resolving it or working around it. Let's begin with recognition.

When you think of conflict, do you envision two hefty gents standing in the middle of the hallway, fists and voices raised, neck veins pulsing? That is certainly a kind of conflict, but in most offices, not one that occurs regularly. There are other, more subtle forms. The following are symptoms that a good communicator will recognize as being indicative of conflict.

1. AVOIDANCE

The most obvious type of avoidance is physical. If your boss ducks around the corner when she sees you coming, or your secretary tries to hide behind the file cabinet, you know you are being avoided. However, there is also the less direct form.

When you telephone an individual a dozen times and are repeatedly told he is unavailable, you are being avoided. When your letters and memos gather dust in the cubbyholes, you are being avoided. You can also be avoided in person, so to speak. This is done, not with the cut direct, but with the kindness that kills. A worker who is overly polite is avoiding getting to the core of the conflict by using manners as a shield. You have probably done this yourself at one time or another. When you are smiling at someone, don't you sometimes envision yourself squishing a luscious coconut cream pie right in his face?

2. WITHDRAWAL

Physical withdrawal was already discussed. There is also mental or emotional withdrawal. When there is a prolonged, unnatural silence following your comments, the listener was probably off in a world of her own, totally withdrawn from you and your comments. When a co-worker is friendly, but not a friend, she is being withdrawn. Note that withdrawal is not always negative. If you have a volcano of frustration ready to boil over inside of you, but you cannot explode and keep your job, withdrawal might be the best (temporary) way to keep your sanity and your paycheck.

3. TENSION

Tension is a sure fire sign of conflict. If you approach your secretary and see her shoulders tighten, her jaw clench, her hands become fists, you don't have to be a genius to recognize that you make her nervous. Do you intimidate her? Does she fear that you will begin yelling, or—perhaps worse—be overly polite with her, with the deadly low voice that indicates your severe displeasure? You may not be aware of a conflict between the two of you, but if she looks strained every time you approach, something is wrong.

4. ABUSIVE ACTIONS

Ah, this is the one symptom of conflict all of us recognize. If one worker constantly punches another, "in fun," there is conflict. If two workers call each other names or make obscene gestures, the conflict is on the surface. Usually, by the time matters have come to this stage of open hostility, there are serious problems.

The above four are the most basic indicators of conflict, symptoms you can use to diagnose difficulties. When there is conflict, communication and networking become very hard. How can you get your message across to a person who is avoiding you, who withdraws mentally from you, who tightens like a spring when you get near? It is easy to see how difficult it is to communicate or work with someone who is openly hostile, staring at you balefully, threatening you. When you see these symptoms, use them as a "call to action." They tell you that you need to work on improving your cooperation, your coordination, and ultimately your communication.

LISTENING

We used to have a boss, an excellent communicator, who had a sign on the wall. Its saying has become a favorite of ours: *"People don't always care how much you know, but they know how much you care by the way you listen."*

So far in this chapter, we have been talking about communication in general. You saw how important it is to effective networking, learned the three elements that make up the process of communication, and read through several anecdotes illustrating the possible obstacles to good communication. To this point, the emphasis has been on the outward direction of communication, on sending a message or talking. While that may be what most of us consider communication, there is another aspect to it as well: receiving the message or listening.

If you are going to succeed in business, you need to understand what you are being told. You don't want to fall prey to the old joke about "I know you think you understand what you thought I said." The consequences of not listening, of misinterpreting a directive, can be costly, both to the firm (which loses money) and to you (who lose your job).

How important is listening? It's been said that 50 percent to 60 percent of all salaries are earned by listening. How much do you listen in the course of a working day? According to several estimates, most of us spend 9 percent of our working day writing, 16 percent reading, 30 percent talking, and 45 percent listening. Unfortunately, many of us are not operating at peak listening efficiency because of poor listening habits that interfere with our ability to listen, and consequently, to respond effectively. Why be a good listener? There are more advantages to listening than you realize. The following are six most of us recognize; can you list any more?

- We learn a great deal by listening.
- It helps us solve problems.
- It gives us time to think.
- It increases our self-confidence.
- It helps us sell ideas.
- It generates ideas.
- _____
- _____
- _____
- _____

As you read the six reasons (and added more of your own) why you listen carefully, did you connect those reasons with people and instances? For example, did you read, "It teaches us a great deal," and think back to your last meeting in which you kept taking notes as a colleague was talking, and thinking, "That's interesting; I didn't know that; I'm glad he brought that up." How do you think your coworker who made the points learned them himself? Chances are, he learned by listening.

Listening is a skill, like any other; there are those who are good at it and those who are not. Since listening is so important, let's spend some time thinking about what makes an effective listener and what makes a poor one. Can you list three people whom you consider good listeners? Why did you select them? If they are simply quiet people who rarely offer any opinions of their own, does that make them effective listeners automatically? How about listing three people whom you consider poor listeners? Ah, that probably was a simple task, right? It's usually far easier to find those with weak listening skills than with good ones.

How about you? Are you a good listener or not? Do you have any listening habits that could be improved? Here is an inventory to help you assess your listening habits. Circle **Y** if you think the answer is Yes, **N** if it's No.

Y N **1.** Do you ever turn your thoughts to other subjects when you believe a speaker will have nothing particularly interesting to say?

Y N **2.** Can you tell from a person's appearance and delivery that he/she won't have anything worthwhile to say?

Y N **3.** When you are puzzled or annoyed by what someone says, do you interrupt the speaker?

Y N **4.** Do you listen primarily for facts rather than ideas when someone is speaking?

Y N **5.** When somebody's talking to you, do you try to make him/her think you're paying attention when you're not?

Y N **6.** When you're listening to someone, are you easily distracted by outside sights and sounds?

Y N **7.** Do you go out of your way to avoid hearing things you feel will be too difficult to understand?

Y N **8.** Do certain words, phrases or ideas prejudice you so that you cannot listen objectively?

Y N **9.** You think about four times faster than a person usually talks. Do you use this excess time to think about other things while you're keeping general track of the conversation?

Y N **10.** Do you refuse to give the other party a chance to talk?

Y N **11.** Do you interrupt while someone is making a point?

Y N **12.** Do you impart the feeling that your time is being wasted?

Y N **13.** Are you constantly fidgeting with a pencil or paper?

Y N **14.** Do you ever get the speaker off the subject?

Y N **15.** Do you stifle new suggestions immediately?

Y N **16.** Do you anticipate what the other person will say next?

Y N **17.** Do you put the other person on the defensive when you ask a question?

Y N **18.** Do you ask questions that indicate that you have not been listening?

Y N **19.** Do you try to out-stare the speaker?

Y N **20.** Do you overdo your show of attention by nodding too much or saying yes to everything?

Y N **21.** Do you insert humorous remarks when the other person is being serious?

Y N **22.** Do you frequently sneak looks at your watch or the clock while listening?

All done? Did you notice one interesting factor about the quiz: It was all negative. That is, each point illustrated an action that a poor listener would do. The more Y's you had, the more you need to work on your listening skills.

We started off with the negative checklist because it is so easy to identify weak skills, so easy to be critical. Let's go now to the more positive side.

For each question, answer Most of the time, Occasionally, or Seldom.

When you listen , do you . . .

_____ Position yourself so that you can see and hear the other person or persons clearly?

_____ Continually reflect mentally on what the speaker is trying to say?

_____ Suspend judgment of the person's appearance and delivery?

_____ Examine your thoughts for prejudice and bias that may influence your reception of the other person's message?

_____ Keep your mind open to new ideas or variations of old themes that might be more productive?

_____ Focus on the importance of the message and repeat key concepts and essential aspects of the information?

_____ Listen to the feelings being expressed to understand the other person's comments better?

_____ Maintain frequent eye contact with the other person?

How did you do? On this second quiz, a good listener will have more "Most of the time" than "Seldom." Are you feeling somewhat abashed now, thinking that you are not a good listener, wondering how much you have been missing all these years? It is indeed possible that there has been much communication that you have been ignoring. If you suspect that to be the case, it's not too late. You can change. Once you have altered your attitude from a blasé one of, "Everyone can hear; what's so tough about that?" to a more productive one of, "Listening takes skill, patience, practice and conscious effort, and I am willing to make that effort" you can improve your listening skills greatly. The following guidelines can help.

1. INCREASE YOUR LISTENING SPAN

Resist the temptation to interrupt. Wait until the speaker has had the opportunity to say what he has to say before you begin to speak. Your listening actions show him just how interested you are in hearing him out, in wanting to understand. If you are not sure of what is being said, or if body language and content of message seem to say different things, ask him to repeat or clarify it. This helps you evaluate your understanding of what has been said. This is especially critical in networking, where you want to be sure you are doing what the other person wants of you. Remember the Max and Alexandra example, where Alexandra wasted a lot of her own time by not hearing exactly what Max was saying.

2. TAKE TIME TO LISTEN

Don't rush, and don't rush listening. Don't say, 'Yes, yes, but just get to the point." How many times have you sat across a conference table from someone who took twenty minutes to tell you one piece of information? You might have been tempted to heave a sigh and say, "Okay, please just get to the point!" but in doing so, you would not only offend the speaker's feelings but would hurt his communication skills. Much of networking consists of asking for favors. It is not easy for everyone to ask favors; most of us would prefer to be in the position of Lady Bountiful, bestowing rather than beseeching. A favor seeker might hem and haw and stammer around quite a bit before getting to his request. Be patient. There will be a time when the roles are reversed and you will be grateful that someone is tolerant of you own verbal fumblings as you gather up your nerve to ask for what seems to you a big favor.

3. DON'T OVERREACT

It's all too easy to get baited into an emotionally charged conversation, especially when your convictions, beliefs, or values are challenged. From that moment on, emotional filters keep you busy thinking up arguments in defense. Most of the time, a networker is seeking something form you, not judging you. As mentioned previously, it is often awkward and uncomfortable for someone to make a request, especially an executive who is used to giving orders. A person who is part of your network is there because she feels she can help you, and you can help her. There is an investment of time and energy, but very little emotion. Try not to overanalyze what is being asked of you, even if it is poorly phrased, like, "I did you a favor last week; now it's your turn to do one for me." Your first reaction might be, "Well, I have been doing you favors for years, and I only asked one small one in return; you have a lot of nerve, attacking me and trying to make me feel guilty!" No, there was no attack, there was just a poor communication.

4. DON'T FAKE ATTENTION

You've probable seen and laughed at television shows in which a speaker is addressing a conference of extremely bored listeners. Audience members are staring fixedly at the speaker, occasionally nodding or making "harrumps!" in agreement, but obviously faking attention. The speaker, aware of this, decides to test his audience by making outrageous statements. "The way to improve productivity is to give the workers 100% of the profits from the products they make!" he bellows. "We can reduce turnover by holding the spouses and children of our workers captive while they are in our employ!" he shouts. The audience doesn't blink, just keeps on staring and nodding. Are you guilty of faking this same kind of attention? Most of us are. When we make up our minds that what someone else has to say is dry, boring or useless, we frequently feign attention. We may fix a stare or let our thoughts wander. Once the disinterest is noticed, the speaker feels rejected and his thinking may become confused. This only prolongs the agony, as the individual is determined to get out what he wants anyway. If a member of your network has taken the time to speak to you, it is usually for a particular reason. If you fake attention and get caught, the speaker will just start all over again, to be absolutely certain you understand what he is asking of you.

5. LIMIT DISTRACTIONS

You can limit many of the distracting sounds, objects, and people unrelated to the situation at hand, such as a telephone ringing. In the middle of a conversation, don't just turn and walk away to answer the phone if it can just as easily be picked up by someone else (If it can't be answered by another, excuse yourself courteously. Don't say, "I don't have time for this, I need to answer the phone," or, on the other hand, without saying something, rush to answer the phone). These messages convey that the other person is not important. Concentrate on what he or she is saying. This is essential in the case of conversing with a member or your network who has called "just to keep in touch." He may already feel that he is imposing on you, since he is not calling about any specific matter or business. If you put the speaker on hold while you get other calls, or chatter with your secretary in the doorway while he is telling you of is latest business coup, he will get the feeling that his call in fact is an intrusion, and will go away with bruised feelings, and worse, yet, the resolve not to bother keeping in touch with you since you obviously don't appreciate his effort.

6. LISTEN BETWEEN THE LINES

Listen to the content but also pay attention to understand the attitudes, needs and motives behind the words. The speaker's words may not always contain the entire message. The changing tones and volume of his voice have meaning, too, as do facial expressions, gestures, and body movements. As Shakespeare said, "A man may smile and smile, and be a villain." Be alert to nonverbal cues. When you are listening, look consciously, not just subconsciously, for the physical actions that tell more of the tale than the words do. When a member of you network casually suggests lunch to touch bases, you may not think there is more to it than that. And there may not be. However, if you are a good listener, you might sense a sense of suppressed excitement that indicates the speaker is just dying to have you "force" him into telling you the big news, or a feeling of sadness that you might benefit from understanding (rumors that a firm is closing or that someone is being forced out).

7. DON'T MONOPOLIZE

A special listening problem occurs when you are the experienced worker listening to a newcomer. It is very easy for you as a more experienced and supposedly wiser being to feel that you already know everything someone else has to say to you. You might be so concerned with helping him understand something that you keep butting in, keep giving more information to someone who is trying to rephrase it in his own words to make certain he understands it. If someone is new to your network, you might be eager to show off how excellent the network in fact is, jumping into the conversation by dropping this name here and that name there. What you are doing is wasting the time of the speaker, who came to you with a specific problem. Even though you are the veteran of the network, you include new people because they have something to contribute. If all you do is bring up what you already know, you are not gaining the benefit of the fresh blood.

ACTIVE LISTENING

The above seven steps give you general advice on how to become a better listener. An even more effective way of responding to a listening situation is called **active listening.** Active listening, as a communication skill, helps people solve their own problems. In active listening, the listener is involved with the sender's need to communicate. To be effective, the listener must take an active responsibility to understand the content and feeling of what is being said. The listener can respond with a statement, in his own words, of what he feels the sender's message means. For example:

Sender: "The deadline for this report is not realistic!"

Listener: "You feel you're pressured to get the report done."

If the listener is to understand the sender's meaning, he will need to put himself in the other person's place. Feeding back perception of intended meaning allows the listener to check the accuracy of his listening and understanding. An open communication climate for understanding is created through active listening. The listener can learn to understand what a person means and how the person feels about situations and problems. Active listening, then, is a skill that can communicate acceptance and increase interpersonal trust among people. It can also facilitate problem solving.

Active listening means attending fully to the words someone is speaking and to the feelings he or she is expressing. When you actively listen, you are telling the other person that he or she is worth your time and attention, that he or she is or could be a valuable part of your network. In the following example, Roberta is an active listener.

Marianne walked into the office where her colleague, Roberta, was talking on the phone. Marianne turned to leave, muttering, "I can never get any work done around here!"

"You sound angry," said Roberta, quickly ending her phone conversation. "Are you just angry, or are you angry at me?

Replied Marianne, "I'm angry because I have a dozen or more calls that have to be made today, and I don't want to make them. I'm not angry at you. I'm sorry for making you feel bad. If you are finished with the phone, I'll begin my calls."

Active listening is a most effective tool. First of all, it is a defusing device: it defuses anger simply because of the acknowledgment given to one person by another. In this case, Roberta's questions made clear that yes, Marianne was frustrated and upset. Second, her listening clarified the direction of the anger. Was it a personal, vindictive anger? Or was her colleague upset about an event, not with Roberta? Marianne was actually frustrated with the task of making a number of calls, none of which she had wanted to place. Third, active listening allows you to decide whether and how you want to participate in someone else's frustration. Roberta has an opportunity to show empathy toward her colleague and thus alleviate some of Marianne's frustrations. For example, Roberta could suggest that Marianne use the phone now since her own calls were not quite as urgent. Or the two could generate other alternatives. The point is, they have an opportunity to preserve their relationship.

Learning how to assess your own listening skills, and how to improve them is certainly a critical skill. You can understand the importance of listening, how it is an essential step of the communications process, a process that determines how well you perform in your career. You can also go beyond just listening, to *active listening*, and the benefits thereof. Listening, however, it just one of the facets of communication. The next one, just as important, is feedback.

FEEDBACK

Feedback may be divided into two areas: giving and getting. Since most of us are more comfortable criticizing and giving suggestions and comments than we are receiving criticism, let's begin there.

Giving Feedback

Michael's associate Brant has not been doing well lately. His many mistakes in letters, calculations, and sales presentations have caused quite a few problems in the office. Everyone, especially Michael, has been covering up for Brant because "He's such a nice guy; I know he'd do the same for me." However, the time has come that someone must do something. The office personnel have elected Michael to take Brant out to lunch and give him some feedback about his poor performance. Michael is surprised to find that he is more nervous as he goes out the door than he was even for his own job interview. "How on earth am I going to tell him he is doing a bad job without hurting his feelings and losing a good working relationship?"

Haven't you been in the same position as Michael? Whether you are a boss or an entry-level employee, chances are you sometime have had to tell someone about the less than acceptable quality of his work. The technical term for informing a person how he is doing is feedback; most of us call it torture.

In the business world, there comes a time when you have to evaluate others. Many managers hate the evaluation period, that time when manager and worker sit down together to discuss how the worker is doing. Some managers are embarrassed at reviewing people who are friends, people with whom they associate every day. Other managers are intimidated, worried that they will lose a good working relationship if the evaluation is seen as criticism. Still other managers are bored by the whole procedure, rationalizing that no one ever listens to the conversation or reads the merit review anyway, so why bother doing a good job?

The reality is that someone *is* listening and reading: the individual who is being evaluated. Few workers have any difficulty giving or getting positive feedback, it's the criticism, or negative feedback that causes difficulties. Therefore, it is essential that one of your communication skills be the adept dispersal of negative feedback. To be more specific, there are several reasons you should hone your feedback giving skills.

1. PROFESSIONAL REPUTATION ENHANCEMENT

Since giving criticism is so difficult, your colleagues will honestly respect and admire you if you are able to do so well. Think about the people in your firm who have your own admiration. Probably one thing you like about them is their skill in dealing with difficult situations. What could be more difficult than criticizing someone to his face?

2. LEARNING

You might think of giving feedback as a time when only the listener, or recipient, learns. Not so. If you are good at giving feedback, and can do so without causing an emotional outburst or alienating the listener, he will probably give you some justification for his behavior, or present you with facts you didn't know. You will have learned because you were able to deal with the individual in a professional, skillful manner.

3. REDUCING EMOTIONAL EXHAUSTION

If you are a parent, you have probably said to your child as you were about to spank her, "This hurts me more than it does you." Of course, no kid believes that, but it is true. The same occurs in business. Often, it is more painful for a boss or a worker to give criticism than to take it. We all worry about hurting the listener's feelings, or going too far. It is common to agonize over the criticism for hours or even days before giving it. If you are good at presenting negative feedback, you save yourself much emotional exhaustion.

4. ANALYZING THE QUALITY OF THE FEEDBACK

If you are not good at giving feedback, you may worry so much about how you present it that you concentrate more on your attitude and tone than on content. Of course, how you say something is important, sometimes as important as what you say, but don't let what you say get lost by the wayside. If you are good at giving feedback, you can spend less time worrying about why and how you are saying something, and more on what you are saying.

Karl got a call one afternoon from the personnel director. "Karl, we are looking for a new radiology lab director. Didn't you used to work with a radiologist? I vaguely recall your mentioning that to me a long time ago. I thought I'd call and see whether you had anyone you could refer for the position." Karl went through his Rolodex and called three old friends of his, all of whom appreciated the referral and agreed to go for the interview. The personnel director hired Andy, and called to thank Karl. Andy also called with thanks, leaving Karl feeling pretty good about himself—but not for long.

About a month later, Karl ran into the personnel director in the cafeteria. "So, how it going with Andy? Is he still doing a good job for you?" Immediately, Karl was sorry he asked. The director rolled his eyes, gave a deep shrug, and said, "Quite honestly, I'm considering letting him go. I think he oversold his qualifications to me. He has done a bad job in the lab; all the assistants are complaining that he simply doesn't know his stuff. The doctors are unhappy too, and really putting the pressure on me." On and on the director went, reciting the litany of problems that had arisen a a result of hiring Andy. Karl extricated himself as quickly as he could and called Andy.

It was apparent that Andy didn't have any idea how serious things were. He knew that he had made some mistakes, but felt that they were just part of the settling in program that everyone goes through in a new job. He was overall pretty pleased with himself, and still appreciative of the recommendation. Karl bit his tongue just in time to keep from telling Andy that it was a referral, not a recommendation. He didn't want to make Andy upset, and felt it would be a little childish to do the Pontius Pilate "I wash my hands of this whole affair" routine. Instead, Karl got off the telephone after arranging to have lunch with Andy the next day. It was time for some negative feedback.

At lunch, Karl began criticizing Andy almost as soon as the two men were seated. Before the bread basket was on the table, recriminations were flying. Every time Karl would mention an incompetence of Andy's, Andy would counter with "You are not involved in the day-to-day business, are not a radiologist, and don't understand the situation." Andy was extremely defensive. Soon, it became clear to both men that nothing constructive was being done. Karl felt let down and responsible for the failure of Andy. Andy felt that Karl was overreacting and taking responsibility for something that was not his concern. As he kept repeating, "All you did was get my foot in the door. The job is mine, no responsibility of yours. I'll sink or swim on my own, so lay off. Tell the director to talk to me personally, not to go to you behind my back.

The lunch was a total failure, no constructive suggestions were given on how to improve the situation. In fact, Andy was not quite certain exactly what was wrong. Karl was more given to abuse than to solid facts. Both men left feeling that their relationship was totally spoiled, each resenting what he was as a wholly improper attitude on the part of the other.

Assessment (or Self-Feedback)

As is obvious from the example of Karl and Andy, knowing how to give feedback skillfully is an art. It is to your advantage to be good at that art, in order to avoid harming not only your reputation, but your network as well. If Karl were a little more proficient at giving negative feedback, he could have righted the situation with Andy, or at least left him feeling that he had not been under a full scale attack. Karl lost a valuable member of his network and gained nothing in return, no satisfaction, no pledges of change, nothing. Giving feedback is not easy. How good are you at doing so? If you can answer "Ha! Not me, I never do that!" to most of the following questions, you have excellent feedback skills. If you find yourself shrinking into the depths of your chair and recognizing yourself in some of the statements, join the club. Most of use are not as good at giving feedback as we would like to be.

1. I don't plan a time or place to give my criticism; I just catch the person's eye and start talking as I quickly as I can. After all, we busy people need to get these things done when we have a few moments.

2. I don't let the other person justify herself, cutting her off with a brusque, "Let me finish; I don't want to hear your excuses."

3. I act, maybe out of embarrassment, as if I am doing the person a big favor by taking my precious time to tell her of her mistakes. My attitude is that I know so much better than she does that she should be grateful for my help.

4. I automatically assume the other person was in the wrong, and expect an apology. If one is not forthcoming, I continue the litany of the person's wrongs until I make her see the error of her ways.

5. I am so emotional when I give negative feedback, so nervous or depressed at having to criticize someone, that I have to fight to keep my emotions in check. This makes me seem stiff and wooden, uncaring.

6. I openly show my frustration or disgust with the person, really throwing my emotions into the criticism I am giving.

7. I let my criticism turn into a personal attack, especially if the listener begins to attack me first. Soon, the matter is more personal than professional.

8. I justify my criticism by beginning with a list of my

qualifications and credentials, making certain the other person is so overwhelmed by my superiority that she makes no attempt to do other than stand there and take my criticism.

9. I underestimate the other person, assuming because I am pointing out a problem or difficulty that she does not know what she is doing. I condescend to her.

Did you realize there were so many pitfalls in giving negative feedback? Sometimes it seems as if it is not worth giving that criticism, considering all the effort you have to make. You might be tempted simply to remove or leave out that individual from your network, rather than go through all that. Cheer up; learning to give negative feedback constructively can be done. The following guidelines can get you started.

1. DESCRIBE THE SITUATION CLEARLY

Identify precisely the behavior that you would like changed. For example, Deborah does not get to work on time and Lois is left with added responsibility. The target behavior is shared participation. While describing the situation, focus on present, not past behavior. Lois would probably like to say, "I'm left with all the work and you get the same pay as I do. I feel like your slave around here!" Such a statement, however, will only get in the way of clearly stating what is going on now. What counts is that Lois is upset because Deborah continues to come in late.

2. EXPRESS YOUR OWN FEELINGS

Two points to remember when expressing your feelings will keep the exchange from becoming an emotional battle. First, take responsibility for your emotions. Lois might say "I feel frustrated and angry when you don't get to work on time." By using "I feel" messages, you don't accuse the other person of causing your response, and he or she is less likely to react defensively. You are simply stating how *you* feel. Second, discuss how you are feeling about the event *without* allowing the feedback process to act as an emotional release.

3. SPECIFY THE CHANGES THAT YOU WOULD LIKE TO SEE OCCUR

Simply stating what you do not like does not guarantee that the other person will know what you want. It is appropriate to ask for a change in the other person's behavior, and the more specific you can be about this, the more likely it is that you will be understood. Avoid being demanding, as this indicates to the other person that he has no choice, causing his response to be of a defensive or aggressive nature. Simply state what you would like to have occur, such as: "I would like to request that you get to work on time."

4. STATE WHAT YOU PERCEIVE TO BE THE POSSIBLE CONSEQUENCES OF A CHANGE IN THE OTHER PERSON'S BEHAVIOR

Tell the other person what the outcomes will be if your request is granted. For example, Lois might say, "If you do your share of work around here Deborah, I will have some help and we'll be able to get the office work done." The consequences, or outcomes, are best stated in positive terms, avoiding "you had better do it, or else . . . ." attitudes. Threatening the other person, while it may create temporary compliance, will not do much for consistent cooperation.

Use this model as a way to prepare to give the feedback: *(Person's Name), I am feeling (emotion) about your (current behavior). I would like to (propose behavior change). If you can do this, I think (perceived consequences).*

Can you see where you could use this in your own life, in your own work? Think about someone who is annoying, someone whom you like well enough personally, but who is not doing the job correctly, who is slacking off, causing your own workload to increase. Go ahead, indulge yourself for a minute in thoughts of telling her what you really think of her,

what you'd like to see happen to her. Then calm down and use
this feedback model to recreate a more professional response.
Write out what you now know would be a productive and
professional, not personal and passionate, criticism.

_____

_____

_____

Done? Evaluate your feedback by answering the following questions.

1. Did I describe the action or situation clearly, specifying
   exactly what it is that is driving me up the wall?
2. Did I state my own feelings, putting the comment in "I"
   terms, taking responsibility for how I feel, not dumping
   the guilt on the other person?
3. Did I clearly and specifically list the changes I want to
   occur? Did I say *exactly* what I want to have the other
   person do or not do?
4. Did I add a little encouragement by telling of the consequences, indicating to the other person *why* she should
   do as I request, showing her what's in it for her?

If you can answer *yes* to all of those questions, congratulations. You understand the concept of giving feedback
painlessly, and are ready to get what you want in a calm, professional manner. Let's go back to the Karl and Andy example
to see how Karl could have handled the situation better. He
had a promising beginning, not blowing up on the telephone,
scheduling a face to face meeting for the next day. Here are a
few suggestions on how he could have kept on that right track.
     First, he could have mentioned his running into the
director, making it very clear that the meeting was an accident.
He does not want Andy to feel that he was being checked up
on. Maybe a story or two about how hard a taskmaster the
director is, what high expectations he has, would soften the

upcoming blow. By talking about those strict standards, Karl is preparing Andy for what follows. Unless he is totally dense, Andy will soon begin to sense that there was a purpose for this meeting, and that what is coming is not good news. He is being eased into it.

Having gotten the courtesies and kindnesses out of the way, Karl is ready to get into the specifics of the feedback. He can tell Andy specifically what the director says Andy is doing wrong, quoting the director as specifically as possible. He should make it clear that he is not judging Andy himself, and that he, Karl, does not know whether the criticism is in fact justified of not. Its merit is, for now, unimportant. The critical element, and the reason for the meeting, is that others are dissatisfied, for whatever reason. If those reasons are justified, it is up to Andy to take steps to change the situation. If they are, however, unjustified, it is important for Andy to know so that he can get to the heart of the matter.

Next, Karl should specify why he personally is involved. It will be logical for Andy to feel that all this is none of Karl's business, that giving a referral does not entail being a Big Brother for the duration of the job. Karl can put this on a professional level, stating not that "You make me look like a jerk for recommending you" but that "It's important to me to know that the referrals I give are the best possible. After all, you wouldn't want me to refer you to a job that turned out to be unsatisfactory, or to send someone to you who didn't meet your demands. I have to think of both parties, you and the director." Karl should take responsibility for his own feelings, making it very clear that whether Andy understands or agrees with the feelings or not, those are in fact the feelings that Karl does have.

Now comes the constructive part. It is not good feedback just to tear down and destroy; the speaker needs to have constructive suggestions to follow up. It is at this point that the listener is undoubtedly very defensive, either blustering in self defense or (if the person is listening to his boss or superior), seething inwardly. He needs something solid and unemotional to hold onto, some suggestions that show the light at the end of the tunnel. Karl can address specific problems and give solutions. If he doesn't know enough about the task to give them, then he might suggest that Andy meet face to face with the director or with the disgruntled doctors to get more information. The important thing is for Karl to show there is something that can be done.

The conclusion of the meeting revolves around the benefits. Karl should explain to Andy exactly how things will get better, now that the problems are out in the open and suggestions are being tested. Karl wants to end on an upbeat note, letting Andy get back his composure and his self-respect. Karl needs to make it clear that he still holds Andy in esteem, and that that respect is exactly why he has taken the time to get together like this. Karl, if he is sufficiently skilled, can leave Andy feeling flattered rather than flattened, pleased that someone thought enough of him to set aside the hours to help.

It's obvious from the preceding material that giving feedback is a skill, an important part of the communications process. Just as important, and perhaps more real to you personally, is receiving feedback. Being able to receive feedback calmly, unemotionally, objectively is critical to your image as a good communicator. Earlier, you learned of the advantages of being able to give constructive criticism. Can you think of the advantages of knowing how to receive it? The following are a few of the most common; you may be able to add more of your own to the list.

Advantages of Receiving Feedback Skillfully ___

1. PROFESSIONAL REPUTATION ENHANCEMENT

If you can stand there and take honest, impartial criticism without becoming defensive, your reputation among your peers is going to be enhanced. Your co-workers will respect your professionalism, be impressed by the control you have over your emotions. They will be eager to be associated with you, to be a part of your network.

2. LEARNING

Although there will always be someone who criticizes you just "for the fun of it," most of the time a colleague who has worked up the nerve to criticize you does so for the best of reasons. Either she feels that she can help you, or (more importantly to her), she thinks that the feedback she is giving you will help her. Regardless of her motives, you are bound to learn something from what a colleague says.

3. REDUCING EMOTIONAL EXHAUSTION

It is truly tiring to have to stand there and take criticism, day in and day out. If you are in a position where you are likely to hear a lot of negative feedback (say you are a programmer, for example, whose programs are always being sent back with nasty notes about "bugs"), the emotional toll can be high. If you constantly become annoyed, frustrated, depressed, or just plain angry when you hear negative feedback, you will soon want to avoid going to work, as it only is a negative emotional experience. Handling such feedback skillfully lets you keep your equilibrium and make it through the day in a much better state.

4. ANALYZING THE QUALITY OF THE FEEDBACK

If you do not know how to take feedback, you will be concentrating more on your own reactions and emotions. If, on the other hand, you are able to control yourself and be a calm recipient of the bad news, you can concentrate instead on the other person. In short, you can be a better listener, and you have already seen how important a communications tool listening is. You will be able to listen well enough to know whether what the other person is saying is valid, and assess how well the other person is presenting her case. You can in fact see the mistakes the other person is making in giving this feedback (Is she too aggressive? Too personal? Too deferential?) and resolve to avoid them the next time you have to give negative feedback yourself.

5. ADDITIONAL ADVANTAGES

(List any you personally have found, or can anticipate.)

_____

_____

_____

_____

_____

   Convinced? By now, you should accept the fact that knowing how to take feedback gracefully is a skill worth having. Ah, but do you have it? The following quiz will help you determine how skillful you are.

ASSESSMENT

Directions: Decide whether you agree (A) or disagree (D) with each of the following statements.

——1. When someone is approaching me with what I know will be negative feedback, I try to avoid the person, or attempt to change the subject, talking first to get the other person distracted.

——2. When I hear negative feedback, I immediately begin justifying myself, buttonholing the other person until she agrees with me that my conduct was proper.

——3. Negative feedback makes me defensive; I assume a contemptuous, haughty, above-it-all attitude, making the speaker feel presumptuous for having dared to approach me with such minor, insignificant gripes.

___ **4.** Negative feedback makes me apologetic; I never question the validity of what the other person is saying, but just begin apologizing and assuming that I was in the wrong, otherwise she would not have brought this up.

___ **5.** Negative feedback makes me so unhappy and depressed and emotional that I sometimes can't stop shaking, and worry I will begin crying. I concentrate so hard on not showing any emotion and embarrassing myself that I don't concentrate on what is being said.

___ **6.** I openly show my emotions at negative feedback, yelling at the other person or breaking into tears and making the speaker feel guilty and sorry for me.

___ **7.** I attack the other person, either for bothering me with her complaints or by pointing out faults and problems of her own.

___ **8.** I question the authority of the person providing the feedback, asking what right or authority she has to criticize me in this manner.

___ **9.** I assume the person doesn't know what she is talking about and tune her out, concentrating on something else while pretending to listen to what she says.

Do any of these sound familiar? Have you taken any of these actions or felt this way yourself? Most of us have. The preceding assessment was phrased in the negative. If you agreed with most of the statements, your feedback reception skills need work. On the other hand, if you felt that most of the statements didn't apply to you, be proud of yourself: You are quite skilled at accepting criticism in a professional manner. If you are going to be part of a network, you will almost certainly be receiving—directly or second-hand—negative feedback. It is inevitable that someone, somewhere along the line, will be dissatisfied with you or your performance. How can we learn to improve our feedback reception skill? The following steps can help.

How to Accept Negative Feedback _____

1. DETERMINE WHETHER THE SOURCE IS RELIABLE

If a secretary who has never seen your work and doesn't understand the technical aspects of what you do criticizes you about your work she may not have the background knowledge required to make a valid criticism. On the other hand, if your boss or a technician who understands the process begins to give you negative feedback, it will be worth listening to. If a person you only casually know gave you a referral and then calls with negative feedback, think about the specifics of the feedback. Obviously, you need to pay some attention to it, because you want to keep the individual as a part of your network. However, the speaker might just be passing on something she has overheard without understanding. In other words, decide how much credence to put in the criticism before you accept the feedback.

2. SEPARATE THE EMOTIONS OF THE SPEAKER FROM THE CONTENT OF THE SPEECH

If the speaker is in competition with you for a big position, he might be smug and self-satisfied when he gives you negative feedback. Naturally, this smugness rubs you the wrong way, and you will tend to tune him out. However, he might be saying something valuable, something that can help you later. Let him gloat if he wants; you overlook the attitude and work on the content. As indicated by the Karl and Andy example, emotions can run high when a person feels that he has been made a fool of or compromised because of having you in his network. Just because someone is not skilled giving feedback (he explodes and goes into a tirade about how you let him down) does not at all mean that you have to be unskilled at receiving it. Separate the screeching from the substance.

3. ANALYZE YOUR OWN EMOTIONS

Emotions are not necessarily wrong. You could have a case for righteous indignation, or for disgust at hearing yourself criticized for something that is not your fault, or for something that in fact helped, nor harmed, the company. However, many times emotions get in the way. Why are you so defensive? Do you deep down know the speaker is right, that you did ruin the job? Why are you so depressed? Do you know that you did your best, yet it was not good enough? Before you let your emotions overwhelm you, determine their cause.

4. LISTEN BEFORE YOU REACT

It may take an act of heroic proportions to hear out the speaker before jumping to your own defense, but try. Some people are inarticulate, have difficulty communicating. They may stumble and bumble and go all around the subject before getting to the point. Others may be so embarrassed at having to criticize you that they bring in extraneous material, criticisms that you heard and acted on months ago. Let the speaker finish so that you are certain you caught the main point. Then, if necessary, defend or explain yourself.

5. MAKE THE SPEAKER GLAD HE APPROACHED YOU

Most business communities are small worlds, microcosms in which everyone hears everything sooner or later. If you are bad at accepting feedback, the word will get around and no one will give you any. This will hurt you in the long run, as you will not learn of your mistakes until you have made them and suffered from them. However, if you make the speaker feel that you thought his information valuable, he will be willing to help you again. A little kindness doesn't hurt. Put yourself in the other person's position: It probably took a lot of nerve to approach you in the first place. If you had to criticize someone, wouldn't you be glad to have that person graciously accept your comments and even thank you for them? This point is especially important in a networking situation. For some people, it might just be easier to remove your card from the file and dump it rather than call and face you with negative feedback. If you have a forbidding mien or a minatory phone voice, you could very well make the would-be commentator feel that it's not worth the hassle. You will then be dropped from a network, probably without ever knowing why.

6. CLARIFY THE FEEDBACK

You learned earlier that it is important to describe the situation clearly when you are giving feedback, to state exactly what changes you would like to make. When you are listening to feedback, do the same in reverse. Paraphrase the other person's comments, making certain you understand them. Help the other person assume some responsiblity, insisting that he tell you exactly what changes he wants. It does few people any good to be told "You have a bad attitude and are scaring away customers." It's much more constructive to hear, "When you raise your voice to a customer, you scare her. Please lower the volume."

Review _____

You have learned a great deal about feedback. You saw how important communications skills both giving and getting feedback were. You learned the advantages of knowing how to give negative feedback constructively, and the advantages of knowing how to accept it gracefully. You were given suggestions and guidelines for improving both those areas. Ready to put them into practice? Try the following exercises.

THINK OF A SITUATION WHERE YOU MIGHT GIVE NEGATIVE FEEDBACK TO ANOTHER

  1. Describe the situation, remembering to be specific and objective. Focus on present, not past, behavior and only focus on the amount of information the recipient can use, not what you feel you have to give. _____

_____

_____

2. Express your own feelings. Focus on sharing this with the recipient and not as a release for your own emotions. ___

_____

_____

3. Specify changes that you want. Try to be specific, but not demanding. _____

_____

_____

4. Share what you perceive as the consequences, or possible outcomes, of the changes that you request. _____

_____

_____

THINK OF A SITUATION WHERE YOU MIGHT RECEIVE NEGATIVE FEEDBACK

1. Describe the situation, remembering to be specific and objective. _____

_____

_____

2. Express your best guess of the other person's feelings.

_____

_____

3. Specify changes you think she might want. _____

_____

_____

4. Guess at the consequences. _____

_____

_____

5. Now, how would you respond? _____

_____

_____

Remember that when someone is critical of you, first use an active listening response: "You sound *(upset/angry)* with me about *(my not getting here on time . . .)*." If the other person responds that this is, indeed, the case, continue with what you perceive to be the problem. "It sounds like you would like me to *(arrive earlier)*. I think that is reasonable" (or unreasonable if that is the case). Remember that if you need more information, ask for it.

Action _____

Let's review for a minute where we are. We are discussing how having good communication skills is essential to effective networking. If you think about it, you'll realize how logical this statement is. Networking involves interactions with others. The better (more effectively and efficiently) you can handle such interactions, the better your networking results. We have covered two essential facets of good communication, Clarify/Affirm Message had two follow up portions: feedback and action. You have already become an expert at feedback (haven't you?) and are ready to move on to action.

Action, in terms of communication, means actually getting your message across. It is not as easy as it sounds. Some

of us know what we want to say, but are too shy or diffident or unskilled to do so. Not being able to tell someone else
what you are feeling and thinking can be a painful experience. Assertiveness skills allow you confidently to confront situations that would typically produce anxiety and frustration
which would otherwise cause you to deny your own feelings
and emotions. Assertiveness skills enable you to assert your
rights without using intimidation or being intimidated and are
useful for managing the conflicts of everyday business.

Think for a moment of the times in just the past few
days when you have had difficulty getting your point across.
Did you become frustrated when you couldn't make a new
procedure clear to an experienced co-worker? Were you annoyed with yourself for not being able to tell a new worker
clearly and concisely and definitely what behavior is expected
of someone at her level, and what behavior is unacceptable?
Did you clench your fists and set your jaw when you didn't
have the nerve or the words to tell your boss that his proposed
project is useless, impossible, too expensive? There are many
times that assertiveness skills could be invaluable in helping
us take action. The following are just a few of those specific
times; can you add to the list on your own?

Advantages of Good Assertiveness Skills _____

1. PRODUCTIVITY

How much time and money do you and your firm waste year
in and year out because no one worked up enough courage
to tell a manager that a project was not feasible, or because
no one could quite put into words the directives that a new
worker, a nice enough guy but confused as to his responsibilities, needs? If you can clearly and concisely, and with authority, state what has to be done and what should be eliminated
from the daily grind, you add to the productivity of the firm.
(*Hint:* As you develop your assertiveness skills, why not keep
an Advantages/Results Diary? Each time you are able to say

what's on your mind, keep track of how your statement helped you, your co-workers, the firm in general. For example, if you managed to make the point in a meeting that sending memos about a project every day didn't do much more good than sending one memo a week updating everyone, make a note of how many person hours and how much money was saved by not having all the excess information. At the end of a week, month, year, tally the figures and see that the information gets into the hands of someone who can appreciate how much your assertiveness has helped the firm.) In your networking diary, keep track of how you have helped others in the network. Then when you are trying to enter a new network, or to induce a person to enter yours, you can casually refer to all those benefits and boons, and have the facts and figures to back up your statements.

2. PERSONAL SATISFACTION

You may have a crystal clear idea of what you want done and how you want it done and when. But, if you cannot communicate that idea to someone else, if you can't override your natural reluctance to dictate, you will certainly end up with another person's interpretation of your job. When you are able to communicate your own ideas, you have the personal satisfaction of seeing a finished task or product that is what you wanted.

3. CONTROLLABILITY

Scientists, when doing experiments, try very hard to control everything but the variable being tested. Although perfect control is difficult, an assertive person comes closer to achieving it than a nonassertive person. If you tell others what to do and what not to do, you are in control. If you don't communicate your desires effectively, you cannot be certain that your own plan worked. Even if the results are correct, another worker might have changed something along the way, done a procedure a little differently, interpreted a directive in a unique manner. Only by knowing that what you wanted done was in fact done can you learn from the experience. This is why we have emphasized the follow up in networking. You can't know how strong your net is unless you test it every now and then. It has to be used. When you are assertive, you have few qualms about calling someone up and saying,—diplomatically of course—"Here's the situation. I have helped you in numerous ways, and feel I am not getting any return. What's going on? Can you help me now?"

4. RESPECT FROM OTHERS

No one wants to be considered an ogre, but we all want the respect that might have just a tinge of fear or awe in it. Wishy-washy people are rarely respected. Think about it. When was the last time you were impressed with someone who seemed to have little direction, who couldn't seem to tell you what she was doing and why? Bosses in particular like to see their faith in you—and the salary being paid to you—justified. If you can assertively say what you have done, what you will do and won't do, you will gain the respect of others. Fellow networkers will soon think of you as a person who can be trusted and respected, someone who will follow through on her pledges. You will have people eager to be associated with you, to be a part of your network, because you are a take-charge person who gets things done.

5. SELF-RESPECT

How many times have you wanted to kick yourself for letting an opportunity to speak your mind pass? How many nights have you sat at the dinner table saying, "I shoulda said . . . ." Like most of us, you probably have uttered the phrase too many times to count, and you regretted your inaction each time and swore it wouldn't happen again. If you are assertive, it won't happen again. You won't glance through the card file one day and think, "Well, I can't call him again because I never told him before how upset I was over the way he handled the

Max Mosher contract," or "I might as well toss this contact; she was so angry over what she saw as my ruining the Carter contract and I never got up the nerve to explain the situation to her."

ASSERTIVENESS SKILLS

You can see that there are advantages to being assertive. What exactly are assertiveness skills? While they are something slightly different to each individual, they have one thing in common. Assertion is owning what you need, including your emotions, and not putting the responsibility for that ownership on someone else. Assertion is also talking about things in such a way that people will listen and not be offended, giving them the opportunity to respond in return. It is a manner that is direct, self-respecting, self-expressive, and straightforward.

Assertion skills allow you to say what you really want to say. Perhaps you know someone who has learned that by shouting, pouting, ridiculing, and being intimidating she can get what she wants. Or, she may have learned that by being a sweet, likable "I'll-do-anything-you-want," type of person, she can get others to respond continuously to her in the way she wants. Whether she is overly passive or overly aggressive, the behavior is inappropriate. To be assertive means to value yourself—to act with confidence and speak with authority.

In the previous sections of this chapter, you were given quizzes to help you determine how effective a listener you are, and how good at giving and receiving feedback you are. Let's try something different to help you identify your assertiveness skills. Instead of taking a quiz, read through the following descriptions and scenarios. While you might find you can relate a little to each one, one scenario or set of characteristics in particular will seem to match your business and networking skills.

The Passive Person

The passive person appears to be a calm, complacent individual who never makes waves and is always willing to do for others. The problem with this type of personality is that such persons are not being true to what they need, but rather are responding to the needs of others. Eventually, passive individuals will feel that they are not of value, that nothing they say has any effect. This often leads to anger, for when passive persons are denying themselves things, they are usually "keeping score" of all that they miss, and just when you least expect it they blow up. You've probably met such individuals. When they finally react unfavorably to something you have said or done, they bring up incidents from weeks, months, and even years ago!

Ron is an office manager. The vice-president of the firm, Jim, often tosses files at Ron, bellowing, "Put these away." When Jim stays late, Ron stays late as well to answer the telephone and run interference. When Jim is not in the mood to work, Ron listens to his interminable college glory-days stories. When Jim has problems with the staff, Ron has to do double duty until Jim has hired a new typist, computer operator, or receptionist. Ron, in four years, has rarely complained to Jim. After all, he figures, why start a fight when Jim is indispensable to the firm, but Ron is not?

The final straw came last week. Ron had a bad cold, but came in anyway to help on the big project. Everyone in the office was irritable, snapping at one other. Ron made a concentrated effort to be pleasant. Jim looked at Ron at the end of the day, and sneered, "Must be nice having such an easy enjoyable job that you don't get tired like the rest of us." That did it.

Ron exploded. He stormed around the office, arms flailing wildly, voice rising. He detailed his job, telling every little task that fell his way, going into the specifics of projects he had worked on three years ago. He quoted Jim verbatim on rude, disparaging, or less than appreciative remarks he had made over the years. He spoke of specific dates on which Jim

had been in the wrong and Ron had saved him without anyone else's knowing. As Jim stood open-mouthed, Ron began to
get into personalities, giving a too-close-for-comfort analysis of
Jim's weaknesses and foibles. When Ron finished, he stormed
out of the room, leaving a bewildered Jim behind, wondering
what he had done. The Passive Person had made waves with
a vengeance, swamping those larger crafts in his way.

Suppose that you have a passive person in your network, an individual who always seems to be there helping without asking for anything in return. Haven't you ever in the back
of your mind wondered, "This is too good to last; when is it all
going to blow up in my face?" How can you best deal with a
passive person to make him a valuable resource in your network?

One suggestion is to attempt to draw out the passive
individual. You are not going to create a personality change,
turning a titmouse into a tiger, but you may be able to get
more information out of the individual. Remember that one
reason you are in the network is to use the other person's
contacts, to pick his brains. If you stiffen up the sinews of
a passive person, he might surprise you by coming up with
information you never dreamed he had. If you let him go on
being passive, the resentments will fester, until either there is
a blowup that catches you off guard, or the person seems to
withdraw from you. We have heard over and over again in
our years of advising people about networking, "I thought we
had such a strong relationship, then suddenly, totally out of
the blue, he stopped taking my calls, stopped dropping by just
to chat, froze me out. I don't know what I did!" Passive people
prefer letting things slide rather than confrontation. It is up to
you to recognize a passive person as such and work at keeping
him involved.

The Aggressive Person

At the opposite end of the spectrum are aggressive persons.
These are the personality types who find it necessary to have
an inordinate amount of control over themselves and everyone

else. They may justify their tactless behavior by saying "Well, at least they know where I stand!" or "I just tell it like it is and let the chips fall where they may!" They achieve their goals at the expense of others. Aggressive persons want to be in control at all times and will do whatever is necessary to accomplish this. Being in control at all times implies taking the control from others, and this is just what they thrive on. The recipient of such a person's words or actions is often humiliated and usually hurt. No one likes dealing with the aggressive personality. As a result, the aggressive person is often shunned and avoided. No one likes to be bullied, and the aggressive person is not tolerated for long.

Amy is the vice-president in charge of sales for a large organization. A tall, large woman, she has used her size to her advantage over the years, developing an almost intimidating way of standing over others when she speaks with them. As a saleswoman, she learned to raise her voice and affect a hearty "one of the boys" attitude in the field. Now that she is in the office, she keeps and even accentuates that attitude. She takes pride in speaking in a voice that is just a little too loud, in being the first one in in the mornings and the last one out at night, in calling everyone's attention to everything she does.

Because Amy is truly good at her job, her colleagues have been tolerating her overly aggressive behavior with few complaints. However, recently Amy has begun to say openly that she and only she knows how to get the job done right, and has begun taking over more and more responsibilities. The others in the office are grumbling at being given so little work to do, complaining that they are treated as children, not as professionals. When Amy comes down the hall now, doors close. After the "official" meetings, there are many "unofficial" meetings to which Amy is not invited, and it is at those meetings that much of the real work of the firm gets done.

Amy has deluded herself that by taking more and more control, she makes herself invaluable to the firm. In fact, just the opposite is happening. A more casual, less structured network is being formed, one that excludes her. Soon, Amy will find that she knows little about much of the work being done. Her overly aggressive tactics have boomeranged, causing her to be left out of the very matters she tried so hard to control.

You may think that your network would be better off without any of these aggressive people. It takes all types to make a network. Some are bound to be overly domineering, pushy, even obnoxious. You don't have to remove them from your network, and thus lose a potentially wonderful contact (in fact, it is just these aggressive people who often have the most knowledge and best resources—being pushy does get them somewhere). You just have to learn to live with them. Accentuate the positive. When you get off the telephone, massaging your ear which is numb from listening to yet another call by this person, remind yourself that one day you may need her. In the meantime, put a buffer between yourself and the individual. Send a card or a letter, rather than have a telephone conversation. If the person expects you to keep in touch by dropping by occasionally (you work in the same building, for example), do so first thing in the morning when the person is raring to get to work and doesn't want to take the time to socialize. The most dangerous times are before lunch and at the end of the day, both ripe times for relaxing.

And keep in mind what your parents probably told you many years ago about obnoxious children: They just want attention. An aggressive person might actually feel a little inferior and insecure, and overdo matters to be sure of getting noticed. It might take nothing more than a few compliments and some sincere appreciation to satisfy this person.

We bet you can think of several passive and aggressive types without much effort, right? Most firms are full of prime examples of each. Are these people friends of yours? Do you respect their work? Probably not. Think of those in your office whom you *do* respect. While they may have some characteristics of the passive person and some of the aggressive person, they rarely fall completely into one group. This type of individual may be considered **assertive.**

The Assertive Person

How do you know an assertive person when you see one? There are both nonverbal and verbal cues.

1. EYE CONTACT

The assertive person uses direct eye contact. This doesn't mean staring someone down and not blinking, it means looking the other person in the eye and holding the contact fairly steadily throughout the conversation.

2. HAND GESTURES

Hand gestures are most effective when they help emphasize the content and importance of what you say. For example, you might pound one fist into the flat of your other hand to emphasize a point. You might hold both hands up in the classic "Stop!" signal to indicate that something cannot continue. Not all hand gestures are effective however. Flailing wildly or making the same gesture over and over and over until it means nothing is counterproductive. You probably know someone in your own office who is a "jabber," one who constantly jabs and pokes and prods you with an index finger while talking to you. It's clear that the action does nothing, just is an irritating habit.

3. POSTURE

Posture can also indicate assertiveness: sitting or standing straight, not hunching over, and not hiding in the corner of a room. When you rise to meet someone who is entering your office, you indicate that you are going to take the conversation seriously. Were you to lounge back in your chair, you would send the signal that you were disinterested, or that the other person could control the conversation.

4. VOICE

Projecting your voice, not yelling, but speaking up and not mumbling is being assertive. It is common to see people make assertive comments and then ruin the effect by either dropping or raising their voices at the end. For example, you might say to a friend in a firm voice, "I want you to be more truthful with me." This by itself sounds fine. However, if instead of waiting for a response you ask, "Okay?" you are destroying the assertiveness of your statement. Other phrases that can detract from assertiveness (particularly when delivered in a whiny voice) are those such as "You know?" or "Know what I mean?" Being assertive involves knowing when to stop talking.

5. OWNING YOUR STATEMENTS

One hallmark of assertive behavior is the making of *I* statements, such as "I feel," "I like," "I wish," "I would appreciate," "I need." The passive person puts responsibility on someone else, often finishing a statement by asking, "Don't you think so?" Statements that affirm what you are feeling and what you need imply taking responsibility for your own decision making. The assertive person has control and has the choice to be more assertive or nonassertive in a given situation. Assertive choice gives you options.

If only we had more assertive people! This is the type of person we all wish we could stock entire networks with. They get things done without being overly bullying. It is usually pretty easy to network with this type of person, as she is the person we all envision ourselves as being. Sometimes, these paragons have so many contacts that from sheer self-defense they have to weed them out. You need to make your network seem so desirable that the individual cleaves to it, even should she forsake all others. One way to do this is similar to the suggestion given for the aggressive person: Show appreciation. Sometimes, this easy going person gets the least attention simply because she does not make waves. She doesn't have to be handheld, like the passive person. She doesn't have to be tippytoed around like the aggressive person. Therefore it is easy to overlook her, figure that "Good Old Connie will always be there." Pretty soon Good Old Connie will be gone.

Table 5-1 shows a comparison of these alternative behavior styles in action.

WRITTEN COMMUNICATION

Although we have been addressing primarily conversation, not all communication is verbal. The larger your network, the greater the likelihood you'll be using written communications. We are communicating right now, via this writing. Obviously, if we were not able to get our message across, if we could not communicate well with you, we would have lost you by now. You'd be off watching television or tossing a ball around with your children rather than reading this. Instead, because we have worked on our own written communication skills, you are still interested in what we have to say, still eager to continue reading and to learn more. (Notice how assertive we were in that last sentence. We didn't demonstrate our latent insecurities by saying, " . . eager you are to continue reading, aren't you?" Ah, it's good to practice what you preach!)

Written communication skills are very important. Right or wrong, we judge people by what they put on paper. Several years ago Anne dated a gentleman who simply could not communicate his thoughts in writing. Even so, he liked writing her letters and did so frequently. It wasn't until after Anne ended the relationship that she realized that his poor writing and spelling skills caused her to think less of him and less of herself for being with someone who was incompetent in this area. Though this example is judgmental, it is nonetheless true. Writing is a powerful form of communication, and a revealing one.

Improving Writing Skills

We want to make you aware of the job you are doing in communicating via the written word. Remember, if you want to network, you need to be able to get across your thoughts and desires clearly. Let's analyze something you have written.

Table 5-1. COMPARISON OF ALTERNATIVE BEHAVIOR STYLES

	PASSIVE (Nonassertive)	ASSERTIVE	AGGRESSIVE
CHARACTERISTICS	Allow other(s) to choose for you. Emotionally dishonest. Indirect, self-denying, inhibited. If you do get your own way, it is indirect.	Choose for self. Appropriately honest. Direct, self-respecting, self-expressing, straightforward.	Choose for others. Inappropriately honest (tactless). Direct, self-enhancing. Self-expressive in derogatory manner.
YOUR OWN FEELINGS IN THE EXCHANGE	Anxious, ignored, helpless, manipulated. Angry at self and/or other.	Confident, self-respecting, goal-oriented, valued. Later: accomplished.	Righteous, superior, disparaging, controlling. Later: possibly guilty.

	Passive	Assertive	Aggressive
OTHERS' FEELINGS IN THE EXCHANGE	Guilty or superior. Frustrated with you.	Valued, respected.	Humiliated, defensive, resentful, hurt.
UNDERLYING BELIEF SYSTEM	I should never make anyone uncomfortable or displeased —except myself.	I have a responsibility to protect my own rights, and I respect others but not necessarily their behavior.	I have to put others down in order to protect myself.
OUTCOME	Others achieve their goals at your expense. Your rights are violated.	Outcome determined by aboveboard negotiation. Your rights and others' rights respected.	You achieve your goals at others' expense. Your rights upheld; rights of others violated.

Find a recent letter or memo, and read through it. When you have finished, read it again, slowly and deliberately, looking for each point discussed below. The comments below are directed towards how an effective memo or letter *should be* written.

1. CLARITY

Be certain you said what you meant to say. You should recall that the first element of communication, whether verbal or written, is having an idea of what you are going to communicate. Check frequently to make certain that you got this idea across, that you have not strayed off the path. Did you use clear, concise sentences that all relate to your main idea? Did you express the idea, give your rationale for stating it, present facts in support, and go on to the next idea?

2. THOROUGHNESS

There are few things worse in writing than an incomplete thought. It is very frustrating for a reader to be going along and suddenly have a thought stopped before its natural end. You know how annoyed you become when someone starts to say something, then is cut off. You want to shake that person and say, "Yes, yes, finish what you are trying to say, what did the boss tell you?" Writers are often so concerned with keeping their material brief (especially in memos or reports) that they sacrifice thoroughness. Check to be certain you have finished an idea, made a point.

3. BREVITY

While too little is frustrating, too much is boring and inefficient. Once you have made your point, go on to the next one.

4. CIVILITY

Why antagonize someone needlessly? If you intended to write a rude, disparaging message, fine. However, for most of us, our communications should remain either neutral and professional, or warm and courteous. Work at using terms that are kind rather than cruel. For example, why not call a report "promising" rather than "incomplete?" You still convey the message, that more needs to be done, yet don't hurt anyone's feelings.

5. VALIDITY

Unless you are only hypothesizing, you want to be certain what you are writing is correct. Doublecheck your facts and figures; have another person check them as well. If you are giving an opinion, rather than a fact, state so clearly.

6. FAIRNESS

Something in writing can be referred to over and over again. Therefore, it is even more essential than it is in verbal communication to give credit where credit is due. If you don't mention in a casual conversation that the idea was John's and your boss finds out about it later, he will give you the benefit of the doubt and assume you merely forgot to mention it. However, it you had time to create a written report and still did not credit John, you look unprofessional, selfish, foolish.

7. NEATNESS

Never overlook the obvious. No matter how well-researched and how well-written your material is, the first thing that catches the eye is its appearance. Turning in a report with White-Out all over it, penciled-in corrections, and torn edges will label you as a poor writer much more quickly than incomplete sentences and misused pronouns ever could.

How would you evaluate the memo or letter you just went through? Chances are, you would like to improve it in one way or another. That memo is history, but you will be writing many more as you become a more skillful and productive networker. To improve your written communication, use the following checklist. Judge each memo or report you write before you deliver it. Your answers will help you to discover in which areas your memo or report writing needs improvement. Answer the following questions with a Yes or No.

CLEAR

1. Are the words the simplest that could be used?_____
2. Do the words exactly express my thought?_____
3. Is the sentence structure clear?_____
4. Is each paragraph one compete thought unit? _____
5. Are all of the thoughts in proper order?_____

COMPLETE

6. Does the report give all necessary information?_____
7. Does it answer all possible questions?_____

CONCISE

8. Does it contain only essential words and phrases?_____
9. Does it contain only essential facts?_____

COURTEOUS

10. Will the tone bring the desired response?_____
11. Is it free from antagonism?_____
12. Is it free from preaching and overbearing statements?
    _____

CORRECT

13. Do the statements conform with company policy?____
14. Are the facts accurate?_____
15. Are the grammar, spelling, and punctuation correct?___

CANDID

16. Have I been fair and honest?_____

17. Have I refrained from being overcritical of any person?_____

18. Have I given credit where credit is due?_____

CHARACTER

19. Is it neat in appearance and make-up?_____

20. Does it truly represent me?_____

Suggestion: Keep this checklist in the front of your Networking Notebook. Refer to it any time you send a memo out or a letter to someone in your network. Remember, that often, by the very nature of a network, you keep in touch only sporadically and sometimes only by written communication. That means that you are judged on that writing. If an individual is important enough to keep in your network, he certainly merits the best written note you can muster. Some of our clients have prewritten, boilerplate "Let's keep in touch" letters that they regularly send to people in their networks. With just a homey touch here, a slight change there, the letter can be used and reused. If you decide to take an approach like this, it is critical that the letter be the best, clearest epistle you are capable of writing.

6
USING NETWORKING REFERRALS TO BUILD CAREER VISIBILITY

*T*hroughout this book, we have been discussing some of the benefits of networking, and what having good networking skills can do for you. In this chapter, we address one of the most common and most important perks of networking: referrals.

When you hear the word *referral*, what is your immediate response? You probably, like most of us, think of a job referral. That is the most common type of referral, and thus the one we will address in this chapter. However, keep in mind that there are many different types of referrals. You could ask for or give a referral about social clubs, activities, and so on. The information given in this chapter, while geared toward, and using examples of, job referrals, can be used for any type of referrals.

EVERYONE IS IMPORTANT

A few months ago, Anne was addressing a group of retired men and women. These were adults who had been in the job market for three to four decades, who had each had a number of jobs. Curious as to what they felt about their careers, she asked the audience in general, "What is the single most valid statement you can make about business?" She had everyone write down an answer on a card. When she collected and read the cards, one response was on over two-thirds of them. It was the simple axiom: It's *whom* you know, not *what* you know.

Many of Anne's listeners had written comments on their cards to expand on the maxim. A few of these are included below:

- "If I didn't have a lot of friends, neither I nor my family would have gotten the jobs we did."
- "The best jobs I ever had were ones that friends told me about in their firms."
- "Every person I meet is important to me as everyone has a large referral network."
- "The best business I have done for making contacts has been at professional organization mixes (Chamber of Commerce, Conventions, and so forth)."
- "I was miserable 'auditioning' for some jobs that were advertised in the paper. I went into them with a negative attitude. The jobs I was told about by friends and associates found me in a better mood, happy not to be just one of the crowd."
- "It's not so much what I know; it's *whom* I know. I heard this hundreds of times, but it wasn't until I was looking for a job myself that I realized the truth of the statement."
- "I have done some of my best business via contacts I made while at professional organization meetings."
- "I have learned not to ignore anyone. Even if someone

herself doesn't seem to be able to do any business with me, she almost certainly has a referral network who might."

- "No matter how knowledgeable about my field I am, in the long run it is the people not the subject matter that make me successful. I think of my business contacts as the lifeline of my professional life."

- "When you have tried everything yourself, it's time to swallow your pride and turn to others for help. I surprised myself by finding that others are eager to help, and that they didn't seem to think less of me for asking."

- "The strongest truism I have found is that people are my most important resource."

And how about you? Think back on the many jobs you have had over the years. Your first job probably came about because of some arm-twisting by your parents. Maybe you had a summer job as a go-fer in the office of a family friend. Simple jobs like babysitting were not advertised in the papers; you heard of and got them through referrals. "Paula has three kids and needs a sitter for the evenings; I'll give you her number and mention your name to her myself the next time I see her." As you got older, you had a more sophisticated version of the same thing. Maybe you had a friend who worked for a firm and put in a good word for you. Perhaps you were dating someone who knew someone whose third cousin had a fiancee whose mother worked for the firm you were interested in. It could be that a professor of yours mentioned your name to a colleague in the private sector, resulting in your getting at least the interview. All the jobs came from referrals.

REFERRALS: WHAT'S IN A NAME?

What is a referral? There are as many different definitions as there are referrals. A referral can be simple, a comment passed along to a friend or coworker that "You should give

Lou Anne an interview; I think she would fit in well with your firm." It might be a little more formal. Your name could be submitted in response to an enquiry. For example, your friend Henrietta was asked to come up with the names of several people who might have the qualifications; yours topped the list. And of course, there is the very formal referral: a note on letterhead stationary, describing your qualifications and demands. All referrals have one important point in common: They create their own visibility. In other words, a referral makes you or someone else aware of a person or opportunity that was there, but not immediately "visible" previously.

SPECIFIC TYPES OF REFERRALS

The following are examples of types of referrals you may have had or may yourself have given in the past. The key to knowing how to work with referrals is to have as many types in the back of your mind as possible.

1. PASSING COMMENT

Your friend Lennie is at a party with an associate who heads another department in his firm. Lennie says casually, "Do you have any openings in your data processing department? My friend Ronald is looking for a new position." Notice that there has been no real recommendation, no details. Lennie has not said anything about Ronald's qualifications, his degrees and experience. He has not said what Ronald's demands or needs are (his salary, hours, vacation time). He has not given any information at all, other than that Ronald is his friend. While these passing comments may seem minor, they can be very valuable. When the time comes that the department head is seeking a new worker, she may call Lennie and say, "Do you remember your mentioning to me at a party some time back that a friend of yours is looking for a job? I have an opening now; how about giving me more information?"

2. REFERRAL IN RESPONSE

This second type of referral is initiated not by you, the job seeker, but by the person who has the job to offer. Judy calls up or sends out notices to several people, asking whether they know anyone who can teach a course in test preparation for the GMAT. Your name is provided. No information is given; no specific recommendation made. The person giving the referral is not obligated, does not feel under pressure to have you perform. Instead he is simply doing a favor for someone else.

3. PERSONAL RECOMMENDATION

This is a more direct type of referral. Here, the speaker knows you and thinks highly enough of you to make an effort on your behalf. She actively solicits a position or a favor for you. Anita may call her colleague and say, "I am sending you the resume of an associate of mine, a young man who has just finished college. Please give him an interview if you can." This is a "higher degree" referral. It carries an onus, both on the one giving the referral and on the one getting it. If you don't perform well, don't acquit yourself nobly and professionally in the interview, you make both of you look like fools.

REFERRALS: THE GOOD, THE BAD, THE UGLY

Have you ever used the expression, "Don't do me any favors?" Maybe you've said after a particularly devastating fiasco, "With friends like you, who needs enemies?" All of these statements illustrate the underlying truth that sometimes well-meaning friends and associates can do us more harm than good. Before we talk about *how* to get a referral, let's examine *what kind* of referral we want, how to distinguish the good and useful from the futile or even harmful ones.

Identify Your Needs

There is a reason you ask for or seek a referral. Identify it. Do you want to get your name out to as many people as possible, anybody, everybody, without discrimination? That would be the case if you were trying to break into a field and had no specific goals, no one division you wanted to enter, no one person for whom you wanted to work.

John has just moved to California from the midwest. He had been an auto worker, but now knows that he wants nothing more to do with cars. He is casting about for interests. He knows that he wants to stay in business and that he has a lot to offer. He is a hard worker, with a good record and experience working both in a factory and in an office. Since he is single and has a little money saved up, he is not too concerned about getting a high-paying job right away. What he wants is to find out what is out there. His goal is to get his name known to as many people as possible, to get a lot of interviews and offers, in nearly any type of job.

John would seek a very general referral. He will take anything he can get, from nearly anyone. It would be hard to identify a "bad" referral for him.

Communicate Your Needs

Your needs may be more specific, more focused than John's. Perhaps you know that you want to (or feel that you have to) stay in one particular field. It could be that because of family

commitments you are going to need a high salary, or to work in
a certain location. *Before* you work on getting referrals, make
certain that you understand your own needs and demands,
and communicate those to the persons giving the referrals.

Adam is a computer technician who is excellent with
machines, but less so with humans. When he has to explain his
techniques, he dries up. He just can't seem to teach others how
to do what he does. He has had many frustrating experiences
over the years of having people comment to him, "But *why*
do you do that? And *how* do you know to do just that precise
thing?" Adam knows himself well, knows that he should remain
in a lab, not in front of a group.

Unfortunately, Adam has not told others of his inability
to work effectively with people. He met a friend of a friend at
a party. In that relaxed social environment, where no one expected Adam to explain himself, to "perform," he was friendly
and outgoing. He gave his business card to his new friend and
mentioned that he was looking for a higher paying job. A few
weeks later, his friend called him up all excited to say that he
had pulled a lot of strings and gotten Adam an interview for a
position as a computer instructor at a prestigious school, one
that was noted for its high salaries.

Now Adam was in a bad position. His new friend did
a lot of work on Adam's behalf, called in a few favors of his
own. He probably expected Adam to be thrilled at the news.
According to the friend's information, the position was perfect:
using computer skills and earning more money. Adam had
not seen fit to mention his lack of interest in working with
people, and since he was so calm and sociable at the party,
his problems didn't come across to the friend. The result: A
referral that is bad for everyone. Adam could just take the
referral, not go for the interview, and hurt his new friend's
feelings and probably nip the friendship in the bud. Adam
could go for the interview and do very poorly, making his
friend who referred him look like a fool, and wasting his own
and the interviewer's time. Adam could go for the interview,
miraculously survive it and be given the job, a job he knows he
would be terrible in. Adam would lose, doing poorly. Adam's
students would lose, having a bad teacher. The school would
lose, paying a high salary to a poor performer. The interviewer

and Adam's friends would lose face for recommending such a bad instructor.

The moral to this debacle is clear. Not only do you have to know your own needs, you have to *tell* others of those needs. Easier said than done? Maybe. It is not easy, and never pleasant, to have to admit our shortcomings to others. Of course you would rather have someone think that you are flexible, can do it all. But if you know that you can't speak to groups, or can't stand working in an office and paying attention to details, or intensely dislike taking instruction, tell your potential referrals so. You save everyone grief in the long run.

Be Certain You Want the Referral

Everyone wants to be the good guy, to do favors for others. Sometimes, we go overboard. You might just let drop that you are considering a career change, and the next thing you know, you getting calls from all sorts of people who say, "A friend of yours tells me you want a job. I own a shoe store and am always looking for clerks."

Rod is a schoolteacher. A few weeks ago, after a particularly rough day, he went to dinner with friends and complained all night long. He had to get it out. He went on and on about his problems, ranging from undisciplined kids to a low salary. More than once he mentioned he was burned out. He never specified a career change, but the implication was there. He didn't ask for a referral. But his friends were listening.

In the next few weeks, Rod was besieged with calls. Concerned friends were telephoning and saying, "Have I got a job for you!" One of the jobs sounded too good to pass up, specifically with the salary offered. Rod went for the interview and was offered the position. However, by that time, he had fallen back in love with teaching and couldn't imagine doing anything else. He had to tell the new firm that he decided to remain in teaching. Needless to say, no one was happy with the situation. Rod knew he had wasted everyone's time and annoyed his friend who made the referral. It was his own fault, too, which made things worse (it always does). He knew up front that he was not seriously interested in leaving teaching, that he was only blowing off steam. He should have made it clear to the callers.

Ascertain What the Person Giving the Referral Thinks of You

So far, you have seen the *good* and the *bad* referrals. What about the ugly? A referral can get ugly when it is more a criticism than a praise of you. The criticism can be unintentional. "Don is a good old boy, never quite got used to the new computers, likes to do things the old way." How will that sound to a firm that prides itself on its new ways, on being up to date and state of the art? The criticism can be intentional, done "for your own good" or "for the good of the firm that might hire you." "Dianne has a bad tendency to rush through projects, not to worry about and pay attention to the details. She is a good manager, but needs to work on completing what she starts, tieing up the loose ends." Would *you* hire someone with that type of referral?

Maria is looking for a job as a paralegal. She considers herself well-qualified, as she graduated at the top of her class. She asks a friend to give her a referral to an attorney acquaintance of his. After she does not hear anything from the attorney, she calls him and asks whether her friend Roger has contacted the attorney. She is told yes, and sent a copy of the letter Roger sent. As she is reading it, Maria is horrified. Every other line seems to emphasize her lack of experience. Such phrases as "recently graduated," "young," "looking for experience," and "eager to start her first job" just jumped out. Anyone reading the letter would not want to take a chance on such a neophyte for this particular position. The referral actually made Maria an undesirable prospect, a poor person for this position.

HOW TO CREATE A REFERRAL

As the above stories indicated, referrals come in all shapes and sizes. How can you be sure that the one you get is good, the best for you? What can you do to guarantee that you come out sounding effective, like someone the firm would be lucky to get?

The key is *preparation*. Make giving a good referral extremely easy for the person who is talking about you. Remember when you had to ask friends to write you letters of recommendation to get into college, and later ask teachers to write you letters of recommendation to enable you to get into graduate school or into a specific program? Most of the time, the people would smile and say genially, "Be glad to. Just write out what you want me to say and I'll sign it." The speakers were telling you that their time is valuable, that they don't want to spend it coming up with what to say. They wanted you to do the background work, in other words. The same is true for referrals. Hand yourself to your contact on a silver platter. There are several ways of doing so.

Put Your Requests in Writing_____

The best way to be certain that someone says what you want her to say is to write it down. If you are looking for a job in not just any old sales but in sales of educationally related materials, say so. If you refuse to work in an office, needing to be out in the field, say so. If you value money more than prestige, say so. This all goes back to one of the points we discussed earlier, about understanding your own needs *then making sure you communicate those needs to others*.

Of course, you need to be careful how you make your "demands." A little tact goes a long way here. Instead of out and out declaiming, "I cannot and will not under any circumstances work for a firm that has no dental plan!" use a little common sense. Say instead, "I find it very important to work for a firm that has good benefits, such as a dental plan." Notice that instead of being negative, you are positive. Instead of putting yourself on a pedestal and saying what you will and will not do, be a little more diffident and simply express what is important to you.

The following exercise will help to distinguish a good request for referral from a weak or inappropriate one. The first letter is an example of a bad request (see Example 6-1). Read it, then go through the explanation of its weaknesses.

Analysis

Obviously, this letter was a grossly exaggerated example of a bad request for referral. No one would ever send out something this bad—we hope. Let's go through just a few of the glaring problems.

1. FORMALITY

This letter is very informal. It is not at all professional, and reads more like a note college students would send each other during a boring class. If you are going to make an informal request, you could do so on the telephone or in person. But if you make a formal request in writing, do a formal job. Cut the chatter and sound professional. "Hi, hope you are doing okay" is college-kid talk, not the writing of someone worth recommending professionally.

2. TOO MUCH IRRELEVANT MATERIAL

The reader of this letter is a busy person. He does not have the time, nor the inclination, to hear about your advanced calculus class or how hard you are working. Use only information that

Dear Josh,

Hi, hope you are doing okay. I am busy with my schoolwork, almost ready to graduate. This semester I am taking an advanced calculus course that is killing me. Oh well, I doubt you want to hear my problems; you probably have enough of your own!

I need a referral from you. I have to get into the job market soon, and have no real idea what I want to do. I am going to have my degree in math, but I don't want to be a teacher. Therefore, I hope you can give me a few referrals for jobs that will be interesting (and of course, high paying!) If you could write me a letter of recommendation to the firms, I'd appreciate it. And send me copies for my files, too, please.

Thanks again. I hope to hear from you soon.

Regards,

Tom

EXAMPLE 6-1

is relevant. It could be relevant to mention that you are taking advanced calculus, if that is something prestigious and could make a difference in your getting a job. However, if that is so, the last thing you want to do is say how hard it is.

3. LACK OF SPECIFICITY

How can the reader know what to refer the writer to when the writer himself has no idea? The writer of this letter is placing an incredible burden on the shoulders of the reader (and most readers would just shrug and that would be the end of that burden, and the end of any chances for referral).

We could go on, but you probably get the idea. The writer is unprofessional, overly demanding, and unspecific. You can just imagine the response this letter will get. It will probably go immediately into the circular file.

Let's try a second letter (see Example 6-2). This time, you analyze it yourself. List three weaknesses, and three strengths.

STRENGTHS

1. _____
2. _____
3. _____

WEAKNESSES

1. _____
2. _____
3. _____

There were several strengths and weaknesses even in a letter as brief as this one. The following are the ones we felt were most obvious. We hope you picked up on some of these; however, there will be others you may have selected as well.

Dear Dr. Samuelson:

Last year, I did consulting work for your firm. Specifically, I wrote the ad copy for your brochure, "The Advantages of Annuities" (copy enclosed). You were kind enough to say that my job was one of the best you had ever seen, and I appreciate it. I really like to get praise like that, especially since I did work very hard on the project.

Currently, I am attempting to obtain a similar job with Dickstein and Daughter. The firm has asked that all applicants submit three letters of recommendation from past employers.

In addition, I am expanding my client list and would be grateful for any additional referrals you could provide. I am enclosing a few of my cards and brochures for your information and hope you will pass them along to anyone you feel might be able to use my services.

Thank you very much. I enjoyed working with you, and hope we can work together again soon.

Sincerely,

Carol Wade

EXAMPLE 6-2

Strengths

1. REMINDER

The writer reminded the reader who she was, rather than just expecting a busy businessperson to remember her. She specifically told of the project she had done, and even enclosed a brochure to refresh the reader's memory.

2. JOB INFORMATION

The reader specifically stated the name of the employer to whom she was applying. This is good; too many writers ask for vague, general referrals. Giving a specific firm helps the writer tailor his response to the firm.

3. MATERIALS

It was a good idea to include cards and brochures in the letter. Of course, you don't want to send along a whole packet, but a few cards and pamphlets can be passed along.

Weaknesses

1. OVERLY UNCTUOUS

While it was good to remind the reader of the business relationship the two had had, it was overdoing it to go on and on about how much the reader had liked the writer's work. If he sees the work again, he will remember his praise. And saying she really liked praise was superfluous; who *doesn't* really like praise, after all?

2. LACK OF REQUEST

Nowhere did the writer come out and specifically make a request. She never said, Please send a letter to So and So at this address. She simply said she needed a recommendation, and left it at that. If you want someone to do something for you, make it as easy as possible. Ask what you want, and be specific.

3. OVERLY DEMANDING

Keep one letter to one request. The ending of the letter read as an afterthought, as if the writer suddenly decided what the heck, I may ask well ask for everything while I am here. If the purpose of the letter was to ask for one specific recommendation, it should have done so, then closed. Additional referrals could be requested in another letter.

You may want to try writing letters of your own. Here are some ideas for practice. For each of the following situations, write a letter requesting a referral. When you have finished, review the letters yourself, keeping in mind some of the strengths and weaknesses you have learned are common. Then give the letters to friends or associates, and ask for their feedback.

- You have met someone at a function, and found out that the person to whom you are writing this letter is a mutual friend. You ask the reader to send a letter to the new acquaintance telling him of your qualifications and recommending he hire you.
- You are switching jobs and want to set up a few meetings and interviews with people in your new area. You are not ready to look for a specific position yet, but just want contacts. You write a letter asking the reader to introduce you to, or give you the names of, possible contacts.

- You are trying to break into a firm that is known for its harsh hiring policies. You ask the reader to send a letter to any contacts he may have, recommending you.

Put Your Qualifications in Writing

To you, the most important thing is your wants, needs, demands, desires. In the midst of your getting all involved in finding a firm that has something to offer you, don't lose sight of the fact that a firm will take you only if you have something to offer it. You need to be sure that the person giving you the referral, therefore, understands and appreciates what you have to offer.

There are two ways of writing what you have to offer. One is general. List your education, your experience, your background. Mention also your talents (organization, attention to detail, etc.). Be certain to spend some time talking about your achievements, such as getting a job done in time and under budget. You could supply a resume, or use the letter to get across the same point.

Cover letters can make or break your referral requests. Go through Example 6-3 and see its strengths and weaknesses, then create a cover letter of your own.

Analysis

This letter is both good and bad. It starts off well, giving specifics. It is very important to say right up front why you are writing the letter, what it is you want. This writer does that, specifying the job. She also says very briefly what her qualifications are.

The letter continues well, telling how she heard of the job and giving herself credibility by mentioning a person with whom the reader has worked. But then the letter bogs down

Dear Sir or Madam:

I am currently seeking a position in your firm as an educational consultant. My strengths are in the areas of speech and writing. I have a master's degree in English and have taught undergraduate and graduate classes for seven years. I have also done consulting work for other firms, such as Benson Associates, Pearson Promotional Products, and Youngs Educational Consultants.

Dr. Greenbaum, a colleague from my teaching days, told me about the opening you have, and suggested that I apply for the position. He used to work for your firm and feels that I would be able to make a contribution, especially with my public speaking skills and experience. (I have done keynote speaking at educational convensions, and have worked one on one with other educational supply firms.)

My resume is attached. I hope that you will find that I have the education and experience to fill the job you currently have open. I hope to hear from you soon.

Sincerely,

Alice Chiera

EXAMPLE 6-3

somewhat. It is a little awkward to say that one is going "to make a contribution." Could the writer have found another way to say this?

And of course, there is one glaring error: The misspelling of CONVENTION. It probably was a typo, but whether a typo or a misspelling, it had no business being in a final letter.

Finally, the writer could have been even more specific. She might have talked about a consulting job she had done in the past, dropping a name or two the reader would recognize. She might enclose a sample of her work. In some way, she has to show what she has done or can do, to make the reader interested and to set her work apart from that of the other candidates.

Now that you have seen some strong and weak points of a cover letter, how about working on one yourself? Create a cover letter for each of the following situations. Then go through the checklist below and evaluate your own letter. Finally, show the letter to someone else and ask for his or her opinion.

- You are applying for an unadvertised job, one that you heard about through a friend in the firm. You are very well qualified, with experience in that precise area.
- You are applying for an advertised job, but are not precisely qualified. You have done similar work, but would need some additional training.
- You are sending a general resume, not in response to an ad or any job opening, but just because you are seeking work. You are flexible in what you will do.

CHECKLIST

1. Did you state how you heard about the opening?
2. Did you mention exactly what you want, what job you are seeking?
3. Did you mention (briefly) your precise qualifications for that specific job?
4. Did you mention your experience in the field, going into specifics about a similar job or project?

5. Did you mention the name of someone whom the reader might know and whose opinion he will respect?
6. Did you send a grammatically correct, professional letter, with no typos or obvious corrections (no white out, for example)?
7. Did you avoid telling your life story, going into too much history?
8. Did you avoid rehashing the same information that is on your resume, instead summarizing or overviewing it?
9. Did you send your letter to the proper person, making an effort to find out his or her name (rather than just saying Dear Sir or Madam)?
10. Did you sound professional at all times, rather than desperate to get a job, or insufferably smug about yourself?

The second way to make your qualifications known is to match them to the qualifications you are aware the firm is seeking. To do so, you need to do your homework. If you want a job with Acme Plumbing and you know that Acme values experience over education, you emphasize that in your letter. If you want a job with Apogee Electronics, which is known for using state of the art equipment, list the various machines you have used and are skilled on. Note that you don't have to tell the person giving you the referral all this background. That is, you don't need to write, "Apogee Electronics uses only the most modern equipment. It is respected in the field for insisting on state of the art equipment . . . . " Instead, just write, "I pride myself on using the state of the art equipment and have had working experience with the following equipment."

Provide Anything You Think the Person Giving the Referral Might Need

Again, the key is being prepared, anticipating the needs of the person giving you this referral. She has a reputation to uphold. Suppose she calls up a friend to mention your name, and is put on the spot with a question like "Does she have anything published in the field?" If your friend has to say she doesn't know, she is going to feel ridiculous. She just may be embarrassed enough that she mutters a quick, "I'll get back to you with that" then lets the whole matter drop. On the other hand, if you have given her copies of articles you have written, she can refer to them and even seem gracious by saying, "Oh yes, I'll send them along to you." She looks good, you look good, and you get the right kind of referral.

THE PERSONAL SIDE OF REFERRALS

1. MAKE THEM LOOK GOOD

Some referrals are impersonal. The person simply takes a letter you sent her and passes along the information to someone else. However, the vast majority of referrals in networking are personal. There is a human being deciding what to say and how to say it and to whom. Throughout this chapter, we have been emphasizing repeatedly, don't make the person giving you a referral look bad. Don't make him look like a fool, lose face. That's a critical concept. What kind of a referral do you think you are going to get if the person giving it harbors antagonistic feelings towards you? He might, just might, be able to be professional enough not to mention them specifically, but they are bound to come through in his tone.

Matthew asked his friend Richard to give him a referral. Richard agreed to call his brother and talk up Matthew's qualifications. Richard asked Matthew to send him a resume and a letter covering what he wanted to say. Matthew agreed to do so, but kept putting it off. Richard called a few times and asked Matthew for the information. The day that Richard's brother called, the information was still not on Richard's desk. When the brother spoke, Richard did what he said he would and gave a referral, but couldn't seem to keep his irritation and annoyance out of his voice. The brother picked up on it and passed on Matthew.

Matthew might have lost a job simply because he made his contact look bad. Richard didn't have the information he needed and wanted. When you ask a person to give you a referral, remember that he is in effect putting his own reputation on the line. Make him look good and he will make you look good.

2. FLATTER WITH DISCRETION

A referral is a favor, pure and simple. There is no obligation for someone to put himself out for you, to mention your name or recommend you. The person you approach knows that it is a favor. He expects you to be a little charming when you make your request, but not a servile toady. There is no need for a long introduction like, "Because you are the top man in the field, with skills I respect and hope someday to emulate, if I ever have that much talent and determination and skill, I am making so bold as to ask you for a favor." Good grief! You don't want the person to will you an estate, just give you a referral. A touch flatters; a ton flattens. A simple, "I know that you are busy and sincerely appreciate the time and effort you make on my behalf" or "You have the knowledge to put me in touch with the right kind of people, the people who can make a difference in my career" will suffice. Of course, flattery depends on the recipient. Those who eat it up should be fed it with a scoop, but for most of us, a simple and sincere thank you will suffice.

3. BE SURE THE PERSON CAN DO WHAT YOU WANT, AND SPECIFY HOW

This goes back to the idea of making life easy for the person doing you the favor. *Before* you approach the individual, check to be certain he does have the contacts you need. It will only annoy the person if you ask him to do something that he either can't do, or that is extremely difficult for him.

Randy runs a small business. He has very few contacts with attorneys, although he has been to a few over the years. He currently has no attorney of his own. What he does have is a niece who wants a job clerking in a law office over summer school break from law school. Because Wanda has always looked up to her Uncle Randy, thinking of him as a big businessman, she automatically asked him for a referral to an attorney. Randy doesn't want to lose any of the hero worship of his niece (he basks in it, has for years) but is a little embarrassed and more than a little annoyed at the request. In order to fulfill it, he will have to contact an attorney himself, maybe making up some piece of business. Then he somehow has to find the nerve to mention that "Well, you see, I have this niece who is in law school, and . . . . " Randy is going to do his best, but the request is not one he enjoys.

Have you ever been guilty of something like this? It is easy for us to think of our friends as having all the answers, as knowing everyone. We have found that people with Ph.D.'s are constantly asked for referrals, as if the mere possession of a doctorate (never mind in what field; it seems irrelevant to the favor-seekers) is an indicator of the ability to make good referrals. Doublecheck *before* asking whether the person has the contacts and can do your favor without a great deal of trouble. If so, he will be glad to help you, both now and in the future. However, if you make the person pull in too many strings and labor too hard, he may do you the favor this once, then screen your calls out in the future.

HOW TO USE A REFERRAL

So far in this chapter, we've been talking about what a referral is, and noting the many different types. We've been highlighting the fact that the term means something different to everyone, as you tell from reading about some individuals who had all three types. We've discussed some techniques for getting a referral, and talked about the subtle personal psychology behind that referral. Assuming that you have decided what kind of referral you want, and have gone after and received it, the big question left is: How do you *use* that referral? Here are some suggestions.

1. FOLLOW UP AS QUICKLY AS POSSIBLE

There are two aspects to the follow up. The first deals with the person to whom the referral was given. For example, if you were referred to Dr. Volk in the personnel office, go see Dr. Volk or talk to her on the telephone or send her the information she asks for ASAP. If someone has given you the referral, act on it as quickly as possible. If you don't do so, you might lose the opportunity you sought. At the very least, you will annoy the person to whom you were referred as well as the person who gave you the referral.

Janice had asked her coworker Al to give her a referral to his former boss, Phil. Within a week of Janice's making the request of Al, she received a telephone call from Phil offering her an interview. Janice was caught by surprise. Being a consummate procrastinator herself, she did not expect Al to act so quickly, nor Phil to respond right away. She stammered a few excuses to Phil and with, "To be honest, I never expected such fast action and I am not prepared. How about if we schedule the interview in a month or so?"

You can predict what happened. Phil didn't want to commit himself to an interview that far in advance (after all, he was interested in someone *now*, not in weeks from now). To make matters worse, Janice didn't even give him the courtesy of requesting a specific date. She suggested an interview in a month "or so." Would any business want someone so undecided? Yet another problem was her comment about being unprepared. Just think how that made her look. She might have thought she was being frank and forthright, but she looked unprofessional. She as much as admitted that she was a procrastinator (a type businesses work hard to avoid), unaccustomed to getting things done quickly. Every signal she gave off was negative. Phil ended the conversation quickly, gave Al a piece of his mind and didn't take Janice's call when she eventually got back to him, more than six weeks later.

The second part of the follow up deals with the person who gave the referral. As soon as you find out that the task you requested has been done, be right there with the thank you's and the appreciation. If the referral were no big deal, just a minor comment to a friend, a simple verbal thanks and an "I owe you one" may suffice. If the task were greater, send your thanks in writing. If your friend did you a really big favor, collected a lot of debt markers on your behalf, make the thank you commensurate with the action. A small gift, flowers, or a dinner invitation would be a good response. Of course, you don't want to go overboard. Remember when we warned against over flattery? The same is true of thank you's. If all that was done was to pick up a telephone and mention your name, sending a huge spray of flowers is not necessary. The poor recipient who sees a wall of lilies coming to his office may feel as if he is attending his own funeral!

Most of all, keep the friend who is giving the referral abreast of what happened. After all, she has a vested interest. If she has gone to quite a bit of effort on your behalf, she is concerned and wants to know what happened. She may wish to know for personal reasons (she wishes you well), or for professional ones (she needs to know how much clout she has, how much weight her recommendations carry). And then again, she may simple be curious (nosey?). If you both show her your appreciation and respect her curiosity, you have a better chance of having her help you again in the future than if you simply ignore her.

Lee asked his associate Margaret to introduce him to her former boss, Brad. She did so, then never heard another word from Lee. She called Brad one day on another matter, and was surprised to find the telephone answered by Lee. It turned out that Lee had been hired, and had been working at the job for a few months by the time Margaret heard of it. Margaret felt rather slighted. While she had received a nice thank you note from Lee shortly after giving him the introduction, she had heard nothing from him since. She had even been mentioning his name to her other friends, hoping to stimulate some interest in Lee and get him new job offers. She was annoyed that she had wasted her time helping a man who had already gotten a job and not even bothered to let her know.

2. DO A POST-MORTEM ON THE REFERRAL

Regardless of the outcome, go back and analyze what the referral did for you, or didn't do. What was the outcome? Was it what you expected, what you wanted? Did the referral come in the form you wanted, or did it surprise you? How would you change it in the future? What will you do differently? Only by learning from your past referrals will you be able to maximize the benefit of your future ones. The following checklist may help.

ANALYSIS OF MY REFERRALS

NAME of person giving referral: _____

_____

_____

DATE I approached him/her for referral: _____

_____

_____

PLACE I approached him/her for referral: _____

_____

_____

MEANS by which I requested a referral (e.g., in person, over the telephone, by letter: attach copy): _____

_____

_____

PERSON'S PERSONAL RESPONSE to my request (How did the person react? Was she flattered to be asked, irritated or annoyed?): _____

_____

_____

PERSON'S ACTION IN RESPONSE to my request (What did she do and how quickly?): _____

_____

_____

RESULTS (Did I get the job?): _____

_____

_____

REACTION of the person to whom the referral was given (Was he impressed by the person giving the referral or by what was said?): _____

_____

_____

MY FOLLOW UP to person giving the referral (Did I remember to send a thank you?): _____

_____

_____

MY FOLLOW UP to the referral itself (Did I call the person immediately, go for an interview promptly?): _____

_____

_____

Let's go through this checklist further to see how you can use it to help you with your referrals in the future.

Points 1 and 2 are obvious. Point 3 is a little more interesting. *Where* did you ask for the referral? Did you mention it at a party or a club meeting? Did you seek the person out during business hours and make a point of putting everything on a professional basis? Some people respond better, react more quickly, if they think they are doing something for a social reason, a favor to a friend. Others prefer to keep everything impersonal, on a business level.

If the reaction to your request was not what you wanted, it just might be because you asked at the wrong place or the wrong time. Pick your locale carefully. For example, we have a friend who approached the father of the bride at a wedding, asking for a referral. This friend thought he had hit on the perfect time, when the father was all happy and giving, full of joy. To his surprise, he found that the father became annoyed and irritated. The last thing he wanted to do at that moment was discuss business! Our friend tried again the next week, calling during business hours, and met with a much better response.

MEANS

HOW did you make your request? Did you pose it as a favor over coffee one afternoon? Did you send a letter delineating what you wanted and what you hoped to get from it? Did you go into a lot of detail or just a little bit? Knowing what you did can help you avoid making the same mistakes twice.

Sharon sent Casey, a good friend of hers from college, a very formal letter on her business stationery, asking for a referral. Casey thought the letter was cold and impersonal, and filed it away. When Sharon called a few weeks later to see what had happened, Casey said, "All you had to do was ask. I don't think we need letters like this between friends. " Judge your audience.

PERSON'S PERSONAL RESPONSE

Did you see the individual's face or hear her voice when you made your request? If she grimaced, it's apparent that something is wrong. Either she doesn't feel she can in good conscience make the referral (in which case you have definitely chosen the wrong person and might get a bad referral) or she simply doesn't like doing such things on general principle (which means that a referral is a bigger deal to her than it might be to someone else, and should be rewarded accordingly). If her tone was warm and gracious, you have yourself a good source for future referrals.

Jose asked Martin for a referral. Martin refused to meet Jose's eyes, hemmed and hawed, and changed the subject. Jose kept pressing, and finally got his referral. It was so impersonal and less-than-enthusiastic that the reader read between the lines and knew that the writer was in fact not recommending Jose. Jose did not get the job.

Deborah started to bring up the idea of a referral to Lea. Lea immediately smiled, and said, "I will be glad to help you any way I can, you know that, but I will need to know a lot more about you. After all, when I make a referral, I am putting my own reputation on the line. Maybe we can meet some time and you can tell me all about your professional qualifications." Deborah, who knew Lea casually (their daughters had horses at the same stables) thought about it and realized that Lea's referral might not be worth the effort. If Lea sincerely did want to know all that information, she might be too demanding and not give a glowing referral. If she was just trying to hedge to get out of the referral, pushing her would make things worse.

CONCLUSION

Although there are referrals in many different areas, we discussed job referrals specifically, since those seem to concern most of us. Some of the best jobs or projects workers can get are through referrals.

Let's summarize creating career visibility by networking referrals using a simple Do and Don't chart.

Do recognize there are different levels of referrals: informal (such as a passing comment) or formal (such as in response to a request). They can be professional (from someone with whom you have worked) or personal (from a friend who knows someone you want to work with).

Don't overlook even the most casual referral; a well-placed comment, seemingly tossed away without thought, can result in an excellent opportunity.

Do identify your needs (know what you want).

Do communicate your needs (let others know; spread the word).

Don't waste someone's time unless you are certain you want the referral; getting a referral just for the sake of having one will annoy the person giving and the person getting it.

Don't ask for a referral unless you are certain you know what the person giving the referral thinks of you; asking for a referral from someone whom you barely know might result in a negative response.

Do put your request for a referral in writing.

Do put your qualifications in writing, matching them (if possible) to the position you are seeking.

Don't forget to include any additional information or materials the person giving the referral might need, such as a sample of your work.

Do follow up on the referral.

Do a post mortem on the referral, analyzing its effects and outcomes.

7
WORKING FROM HOME

*T*here is a Spanish proverb that states, "Be careful what you ask for; you might get it." Remember when you peered over the stacks of paperwork on your desk, rolled your eyes at the overflowing memos taped to every available surface of your chair, telephone, and family pictures, and wished fervently that you could just stay at home and work from there? Remember when you listened to interminable gossip from the office transmitter, shared yet another soggy sandwich with the same old co-workers, heard the same old stories, and wished you could be working at home, lunching graciously and not being regaled with stories of overly demanding bosses and who's job hunting where?

Now you have your wish. You are working at home. You have no one coming in every few minutes to update you on the office romance, no one surreptitiously passing you notes (shades of high school!) about the possibility of your securing the promotion, no one calling you to hypothesize about a merger. You have the peace and quiet and solitude you so yearned for—perhaps too much solitude?

Do you feel out of things, away from the hustle, bustle, and grapevine of the office? As we discussed earlier, information is power. If you no longer are receiving that information, you lose power. It is important to keep in touch, not just with the people you know personally (your former office mates), but with the industry as a whole. It is in the office that you get much information about your career field, what break-throughs are happening, what products are in development, what legal changes are being supported and which contested. And there is of course that people aspect as well: If you don't hear the rumors about a job bid, you can't prepare a presentation until the last minute, submitting a product not nearly as professional as that of a worker who got the inside story a month ago. If you don't know who is angry with whom, who is spatting and feuding, you might put your foot in your mouth, making a mistake by praising one individual's work to another and gaining antagonism. You might be in a situation like Ryan's.

Ryan is a teacher. Several months ago, tired of working in the regimented classroom situation, he quit his job and became a private tutor. He advertises in the local paper for students, but gets most of his business from referrals. At first, Ryan enjoyed working from his home.

"The first month was great. I woke up when I wanted to, took only as much business as I wanted, did pretty much exactly as I liked. But then, I noticed that the number of students was dropping off. The longer I was away from the classroom, the fewer students I came into contact with. They and their parents didn't remember me or didn't think of me when the kids needed help. When I was a classroom teacher, I did private tutoring on the side. Since I saw the kids daily, it was easy for me to get business. Then, the teacher who took over from me also got most of my business. I needed to get my name out there.

"As the months went by, I became more and more out of things. I didn't know about the new teachers who came into my former school. I didn't know who retired, who got a good review, who was fighting with the principal. I was afraid to say anything to anyone for fear I would step on some toes or praise a bitter enemy."

Ryan has decided to go back to the classroom. He gave up, feeling that the isolation of working from his home was too extreme. Fortunately, not everyone has to give in to these feelings. Whether you are just thinking about working from your own home or are actually doing so, this chapter can help you create, maintain, and gain the most from a network.

For example, there is the success story of Jennifer. She quit a good job as a computer programmer to become a consultant. She built up a business going around to firms, showing employees how to operate canned (prewritten) software, and writing personalized or customized programs as needed. Most of her work, the actual writing or evaluating of the programs (some she had to learn before she could teach them) was done at home. Yet, because Jennifer was able to network efficiently, she continued to draw in clients and get enough business to make a living and enjoy her new, expanded career. The difference between Jennifer and Ryan was that Jennifer's net was working.

THE EFFECTS OF ISOLATION

Ryan's story mentioned briefly some of the effects of working from your home, a few negative results of being isolated. Let's examine these more closely. If you are working from home, or know of someone who is, you no doubt will be able to add a few of your own to the list.

Note: Please don't think that we are overly critical of working from your home. Doing so can be advantageous for many reasons. We emphasize the negatives to call your attention to things that you might have instinctively suspected, but have never been able to name. Recognition of any problem is the first step towards solving it.

1. ADVANCE INFORMATION

When you are in an office, you learn things before outsiders do. You probably hear of job openings (in fact, some firms are required to post notices internally before advertising externally). You find out about the possibility of a merger, of a sell-out, of a change of any sort. You can use that information to plan your future. For example, if you know that a business is going to be phased out, you might consider helping those who will soon be out of jobs. A luncheon date, a few names and phone numbers of recommended job search firms, and a little sympathy can go a long way and be remembered when that individual later gets another job and is in a position to help you.

When you work from your home, the grapevine isn't there. If you do not network and keep the channels open, you don't hear the information. You are no better than one of the general public, one of the masses. There are definite advantages to be gained by having insider information (one reason the Securities and Exchange Commission frowns upon it). Stores send their most valued customers notice of sales before they are advertised. Companies offer stock to their own employees before the general public. If you know about these opportunities, you can plan accordingly. Even if you are not a member of the firm yourself, you can arrange for someone who is to purchase stock for you. If you don't work for a company, networking may garner you an invitation to its Christmas party, to a retirement party, to a luncheon. All of these are opportunities to talk and listen, to gain that insider advantage. Besides oral communication, there is the written word that makes a difference when you are in the office. Companies often subscribe to several industry newsletters which employees can read in the library or lounge. The firms send out newsletters of the latest developments, or put notices on bulletin boards. When you are away from the office, you lose touch not only with the people and what they have to say, but with the physical plant and what the environment has to offer. (How can you know whether the new computer system is for you unless you have hands on experience with it? All the conversation with your friend who has one will never take the place of a few hours on line yourself.)

2. FEEDBACK

When you work in an office, you feel the repercussions of an action. If a job you do is adequate rather than excellent, you learn quickly. You may not be told directly that your job was not superior, but the attitudes and reactions of those who were affected by your performance will give you the feedback. You can hear through the office grapevine what others think of your work. If you learn, for example, that everyone felt that the diagnostic portion of your report was excellent but the recommendations were weak, you know what you need to work on.

When you are isolated from the office environment, you get only the most formal, required feedback. You may get a paycheck or a letter, without any analysis of your project. If you are not asked to do a second project, you don't know exactly what it was about the first one that displeased its recipient. If you *are* asked to do a second one, you don't know what it was about the first one that pleased its recipient. You don't know whether the tone of the report was too frivolous or not lighthearted enough. You don't know whether the report was grudgingly accepted or used as a model for others. You don't see whether the report was circulated, was posted on the bulletin board, was quoted in the newsletter. You just plain don't know what was done with it.

3. POWER PLAYS

Every business, every office, has its power structure. If you want to do business with a firm, it is important that you know or at least have some inkling where the real power resides. We have all heard stories about executives who are figureheads buttressed by their hard working secretaries who do everything their way and simply require a rubber stamp approval from the higher-ups. If you have worked in an office before, you know that there is a chain of command that must be followed. You need to submit ideas to person A, then B, and then C. Going out of order can sabotage the whole project.

When you work from home, you lose track of the power structure. If a secretary leaves and a new one is hired, will the new one wield the same power as the former? Has an executive taken an assertiveness course and suddenly decided he wants to be more involved in everything? Has a worker determined to get a promotion and thus committed herself to doing the work of several people, insisting that she be consulted for things that normally would be delegated? If you don't know where the power lies in a firm, you waste time, money, and effort going through the wrong channels. You also risk antagonizing those whose help you most need.

4. PERSONALITIES

Our personalities play an important role in our careers. If an individual is a carefree, easygoing person, his work is likely to be less meticulous than that of a more somber, "life is real, life is earnest" type. Both can do excellent, but different, work. If you work in an office, you get a feel for the type of person an individual is, what type of work she would most appreciate. You don't have to be told, you simply observe.

When you work in isolation, you have no opportunity to observe. You can't tell whether the "Ms. Engleberg" who signs your contract for free-lance work wants everything done by the book in triplicate, or would be irritated and annoyed at having to wade through anything but the essentials. You don't know whether the recipient of the report wants you to phrase everything as if the work were yours, or is a credit hoarder who would be more likely to send more work your way if your phraseology indicated the ideas were hers.

5. WAR

Heaven forbid you should send a letter soliciting work to Dr. Ewing and say, "I have worked with and have the strong recommendation of Dr. Cohen" when Dr. Ewing is fighting with Dr. Cohen. Your letter might not be dropped in the circular file automatically, but it will leave a bad taste in Dr. Ewing's mouth and probably not be considered as favorable as one in which you stressed your recommendations by others. When you are in an office or business environment, gossip lets you know who respects whom, who is fighting with whom, who can't stand to hear whose name without exploding. You know what toes to avoid.

When you work alone, you don't get this information. Very few professionals send out letters giving notice of a falling out. Not too many people tell you on the telephone whom they have fought with lately. Most of us are too ashamed of our sometimes petty squabbles to let others in on them. However, just because they are petty does not mean they aren't real, leaving real hurts and grudges.

6. GIVING

If you expect to take from others, you know there is a time when you will be called upon to give. When you are in an office, you constantly do small favors for others. Do enough of those small favors and you find you are owed a large favor, such as a recommendation or an inside tip. Part of networking is doing for others, as well as having them do for you.

Working at home, you don't have the chance to do quite so many favors. Because you don't know whose adolescent is looking for a summer job, you don't talk to your husband and see whether his firm has an opening. Because you aren't aware that someone is considering going back to school, you don't offer to have lunch with her and tell her all you learned about applying for financial aid. Because you don't know of others' needs, you can't take action to help fulfill them.

We hope you're not depressed by all this. The point of the above is to get you thinking about how important the working environment is, how much it offers to you in the normal course of affairs. As with everything else with which we are familiar, we take the office for granted. Now that you are working away from an office, you should recognize that you have lost some opportunities, some benefits (although you have undoubtably gained many others, sanity not the least among them). It is only when you identify those lost advantages that you can use your network to regain them, or to substitute others for them.

Bonus! Does this situation match yours? If you are interested in more information about working and networking from home, we can recommend a few good books on the subject. Check the Suggested Reading Appendix at the end of the book. *Working from Home*, in particular, is one of our favorites.

REMAINING IN OR TAPPING INTO AN ESTABLISHED NETWORK

The office has many networks. Some are formal, sponsored by the corporation. For example, some firms have "interoffice mail," computers that are hooked up and serve as bulletin boards on which workers may leave any messages they like. Some networks are informal, a group of workers getting together for lunch and talk once a week. Have you lost your chance to be part of those networks? Not necessarily. You can still be an important, if slightly removed, participant.

If you used to work at the firm with which you want to network, make the effort to continue to be part of the informal network. Since you work at home and your time is your own, why not meet those same colleagues for lunch one day a week? Sure, you'll have to disrupt your day, perhaps drive some distance, schedule your work around their lunch hour, but meeting your friends can keep you current. If you sense that your former colleagues are slightly reluctant to get together with you because you are no longer part of the team, give them an enticement. Invite them to your place for a homemade lunch (better than fast food any day, especially when the workers go to the same places constantly and are tired of them). Make reservations at an untried spot and pick up everyone at the office. Pack a picnic and take it to the office, eating on the lawn or in a nearby park. The idea is to make seeing you and being with you interesting and exciting for the workers. The two way exchange of information, the networking process itself, can be fun and exciting as well.

Suppose things just don't work out and that you can't make lunch with your former co-workers or that they don't want to lunch with you. Can you arrange after work activities? Many people enjoy exercise. You can invite everyone to aerobics, to the pool, to the track for a walk. You probably can talk during exercise, but if not, be sure to go somewhere for a snack afterwards to get the inside chatter. Throw a networking party and invite everyone. If all else fails, write chatty letters to your friends. Out of a sense of obligation (how many of us can stand not to respond to a personal letter?) they will write back, telling you what is going on in their lives.

You may be too far away from your former employer to keep in physical touch with the workers. Use the telephone. It's worth the long distance charges to hear what's going on. If you are really sly, you will call at a time when you know something frustrating has happened. For example, we have called friends right before merit reviews. These friends were nervous about being evaluated, and in the mood to talk at length about what was good and bad about the firm. You might want to call right after a major project has been completed, when everyone is in a good mood, ready to kick back and relax and talk for a while.

As mentioned earlier, letters are a good way of keeping in touch. One friend of ours uses a round robin approach. Several friends who used to work together have all gone on to new jobs. Once a month, our friend begins a letter and sends it. The second person reads it, adds her part, and sends it along. The letter continues its rounds, each person adding something, until everyone has seen it. This letter has been going on for years now, keeping everyone in close contact. Our friend vows that someday she is going to publish her letter "because it is a ready made novel, full of suspense, intrigue, and double dealing!"

You can keep in a network by asking others to send you copies of the company newsletter. While you were working at the firm, you probably regarded the newsletter as confetti fodder, but it's amazing how much an outsider can learn from it. If you can subscribe to the newsletter, do so. If not, bribe a friend to send you copies. If you send the friend a self-addressed, stamped envelope that arrives the day the newsletter comes out, he probably won't mind slipping the newsletter into the envelope and sending it along. Make doing so as easy as possible for him, to ensure he continues to help without resentment.

You might be able to continue to attend company functions. If you can be taken along as a guest, ask a friend to take you. You can go to luncheons for retiring people, to birthday parties, to office holiday parties. Even if you have not worked for the firm for a while, if you go to the functions enough, you will be accepted as a part of the festivities.

Suggestion: Keep track of what contacts you want to maintain with your former co-workers. Make notes on your calendar. Sit down now and put the notices at the intervals you deem appropriate. For example, if you want to remain very close to a worker, put a note to call her every week. If you simply want to keep in casual contact, make a note to call every few months, or even just once or twice a year. You have to decide how much time and effort this link in your network is worth, then remind yourself to make that effort. It's always easy to let a month or a year or more go by between calling or writing or getting together with someone. Because you work at home, you may not meet many new people. Therefore, you think constantly about your old friends and have them in the forefront of your mind. Those friends, working in an office, meet dozens of new people and may rarely think about you.

There's no time like the present for developing good habits. Here's an exercise to help you decide with whom you want to remain in contact, why, and how. (See Table 7-1.)

In Column A, list the persons with whom you want to remain in contact, or with whom you want to resume contact. These may be friends and associates from business organizations or competing firms. They may be friends of friends whom you would like to get to know better. Rack your brain to think of everyone about whom you have said, "You know, I really

Table 7-1. KEEPING IN TOUCH

A PEOPLE	B MOTIVATION	C ACTION
Tom Wade	Tom has a lot of contacts at Church Industries; I might be able to meet someone there who can give me some consulting work.	Call Tom and ask him to lunch; meet with him the last Friday of every month for lunch.
Carol Hickey	Carol is president of the professional organization and has great contacts; she can recommend me to a lot people.	Offer to meet with Carol before the organizational meetings to give her some help; get together at least once a month.

should give a call to or get in touch with . . . . I bet we could do some business together."

In Column B, specify *why* you want to get in touch or remain in touch with that person. In other words, list what you want from that person. For example, you might want an introduction to someone that person knows, or an in at that person's company, or simply to pick the person's brain. Be as specific as possible. This helps you see how important it is to be with that person. For example, if the only reason you want to stay close to Nancy is that she is a friend of Dr. Belch, and Dr. Belch no longer is working in your field, you might not have any need for the relationship with Nancy either. It may sound a bit cruel, but be realistic. Since your time is limited, you want to spend it maintaining contact with those who can help you.

In Column C, list what you are going to do to resume or to maintain contact with the person. Again, be specific. You might make a telephone call once a week on Tuesday afternoons. You might have lunch once a month. Whatever the plan, write it down and then follow through. By thinking of what activities you want to share (Can you go to the professional organization meeting together? Can you carpool to work? Can you attend a seminar together?) you take a step towards actually *doing* (rather than just thinking about doing) those things. Good intentions are not enough.

Here's another exercise for you. Suppose that you have been out of touch with someone for too long. It often seems that the longer we put off something, the harder it is to do. It can be embarrassing calling someone after six months' silence, especially if you want something from that person. A little telephone role playing can help. Go through the following, and think of what you would say in each case. How would you respond? By practicing before the situation actually arises, you become more comfortable.

1. You telephone Max, whom you used to be good friends with but with whom you had a falling out. You want to resume at least a telephone relationship. He responds coolly, asking you what you want.
2. You run into a person you used to do business with

when she worked for Dynamo Industries. You are considering changing jobs to go there, and want to resume
the relationship. You telephone her office at the end of
the day and ask whether she wants to have lunch with
you the next day. She is suspicious of your motives,
wondering what you want from her.
3. You never returned the calls from Gerry, who asked
you for some information last year. Now you need help
from him, and you give him a call. He teases you about
ignoring him and asks why he should do something for
you now.

ESTABLISHING A HOME NETWORK

Let's shift gears here and assume that you are not connected
to any particular firm. Maybe you have never worked in a
business office, or worked in one long ago, in another state
or country. You want to start from scratch and establish a
network from your home. What do you do?

1. DETERMINE YOUR NEEDS

Why do you want a network? When you work out of an office
in your home, you need a network to avoid isolation. It is
very easy, when you are not going into an office every day, to
become withdrawn, to get out of the mainstream. A network
can keep you in touch. Do you need to get recommendations,
like an interior decorator who needs testimonials from former
clients? Do you need to get referrals to get business, like a
private tutor? Do you need to keep abreast of changes in
the field, like a writer on technical topics? There are dozens,
hundreds of reasons you need a network. List as many of them
as possible.

Don't expect this list to spring full blown from your

mind. Keep a card handy to jot down more and more reasons you want a network as they occur to you. You may learn from experience that you could really have used a connection in a certain instance. You might learn from the experiences of friends. Be as specific as possible. Instead of writing, for example, "I need a network to send business my way," write, "A network would allow me to meet more people and get my name out in front of the public, resulting in my getting more calls. I could go to meetings of groups and organizations and pass out my cards."

Your reasons are your own. They may be professional or personal. If you work out of your home, you could be lonely and feeling too isolated for comfort. Just for your peace of mind, to feel still a part of the "real world," to feel useful and necessary, you may want to stay in a network. You just might be a sociable type who enjoys hearing from others. There are no right or wrong reasons to network, only *your* reasons.

2. IDENTIFY YOUR RESOURCES

You want to know just where you stand right now. What contacts do you already have? Whom do you know? Do you have friends or associates who know a wide group of people? We have a friend who works from her home but is friends with a college professor who meets hundreds of new students every year. The professor is a strength of the homeworker's network, a strong link.

You are your best resource. Remember that when you network, you are going to be offering what you have in exchange for what someone else has. So what *do* you have? What can you offer, personally and professionally? What skills and talents do you have? Can you communicate well, write a good letter, scan a report and find its grammar problems? You'd be surprised at how many people can't do so. Are you analytical? Can you listen to a speech and find the inconsistencies? *Skills and talents* does not mean just the traditional cubby-holed, titled ones like accounting, painting, and so on. Your character traits help determine your skills and talents. Maybe one of your skills is diplomacy, getting bad news across in a sympathetic, undramatic way. There are many individuals who could use someone like you. Perhaps your talent lies in knowing how to plan and organize. You could be the type of person who tells others, "Okay, this is how to begin: take these three steps first . . . ." Although the others do the work themselves, they will value you highly for being able to see the whole picture, to know how to get started.

What physical advantages do you have? Are you near a school whose library is excellent? You can go there and look up information for someone who is too busy or too far away to do so. Do you have a computer? Many people would love to have you in their network, if for nothing else than for keeping their resumes on your disks (some businesses do just that, and charge significant sums for it). Do you have a large vehicle? If you have a truck or van or good sized car, you can be of help to someone with a little two seater. And of course, a good card file is manna from heaven to many.

3. IDENTIFY YOUR MISSING RESOURCES

At this point, you have identified *what* you want and *why* you want to network from home. You have identified what you *have*. Now, put the two together and find out what you do *not* have. If you want to use a network to gain access to specialized information, you have the knowledge necessary to interpret and understand that information. What you don't have is the ID card to get you past the guardian of the gate at the library or the letter of permission to look at a secured section. Missing resources can be physical (you are the one who needs a truck), emotional (you want someone who can view something dispassionately, something to which you are too close to see objectively), or professional (you need a lobbyist, like a secretary, to get you an appointment with a hard to reach person).

Does some of this sound familiar? These three steps are fundamental to starting any network. However, they may be more difficult for those working out of their homes than for those already in the business community. For example, when it comes to listing your resources, you might think you have none since "all I do is sit at home all day and wait for the telephone to ring." You may want to reevaluate. You have more than you think.

Bernie is retired from a job as a fire fighter. For years, woodworking has been his hobby. He has made toys and gifts for friends. Since he has been retired, he has made so many wood products that his friends are urging him to sell them, to set up a business. Bernie is considering the idea, but has no idea where to begin. He wants to work in his home, not go out and beat the pavement making sales. He would prefer taking orders for custom toys. Bernie thinks that he would enjoy making just a few toys at a time for special people who know exactly what they want.

Bernie decides that he needs help. He wants to network with others to make contacts with people who would buy his products and who would recommend him to their friends who would then place custom orders. He sits down to take the first three steps mentioned in this section.

1. DETERMINE MY NEEDS

I need people to find out that I have wood products to sell. I need people to buy those products then place orders for more. Therefore, I need advertising. I can't afford standard ads in the papers. I could use free ads, if I knew how to get them. I also need someone to handle the business side of this, to help me set my prices, figure out the taxes, get the necessary sales licenses. I guess I need an office manager, someone who will take all the paperwork off my shoulders and let me do just the woodworking.

2. IDENTIFY MY RESOURCES

What do I have? I have a lot of talent in woodworking. I can make the toys quickly and well. I could trade my woodworking services to others for their services, like hanging doors or making cabinets in exchange for advertising.

I have equipment. I have all sorts of power tools that others might not have, including some very sophisticated ones. I have space where others could use those tools. I also have storage space where someone could put packages or boxes or even a small car.

I have time. Since I am retired, I can spend as much time as necessary on a project. If someone wanted my help in a network, I could spend the day making calls or walking around handing out fliers or answering questions. I could use my number as a message center, taking calls for others. Since I am home all day, I could accept packages or letters for others too.

I have patience. I can do a task for as long as necessary, repeating it over and over. If someone needs some "busywork" done, like stuffing envelopes, I can do it without getting bored or irritated.

I have contacts in the fire department and a few in the police department. I know a lot of hospital personnel as well, from my time as a paramedic. I have fire fighting knowledge, enough to lecture to groups (such as elementary school kids) or to give seminars on fire safety.

3. IDENTIFY MISSING RESOURCES

I know no one in sales or in advertising. I don't know anyone in reporting either. I know no writer who can create a good brochure describing my products. I don't know many people with children who would enjoy my toys. I don't have any office equipment per se, like a typewriter or computer or file cabinets.

GETTING DOWN TO BUSINESS

Where are you now? We have been discussing the disadvantages of working from your home and how to identify them. We've talked a little about how to overcome those disadvantages. Perhaps you have already made a start on establishing a network out of your home based on your career and personal goals, or you have seen how one home worker has begun his own network. Now it's time to talk about flocking together with other rara aves like yourself: your fellow homeworkers.

CREATE A HOME NETWORKER'S CLUB

Humans are essentially gregarious beings. Put two of us nearby and we will create a club, complete with funny head-pieces and secret handshakes. You are not the only one who works out of his or her home. Many others are in the same position and would enjoy meeting with you. Why not start a support group of sorts, a club that turns into an effective net-work?

1. LET THEM KNOW YOU'RE HERE

You can get started by getting the word out. Be logical here. It would not do much good to tell all your friends in the business world that you are starting a home networking club. After all, those people are not working at home, but in offices. Instead, spread the word where those who work in their homes visit or congregate. Libraries are excellent. Many homeworkers visit libraries almost daily to work or to find information. Most libraries have bulletin boards; create a notice and post it.

Homeworkers might have more time than office work-ers to read a paper carefully. Find the local, small papers and put notices in them. You probably will have more luck in deal-ing with an editor at the *Small Valley Neighborhood Gazette* that at the city-wide *Post* or *Star* or *Times*. A local paper might write you up, do a profile of you and what you want to ac-complish with a home network. That type of publicity would result in your getting numerous inquiries about your new organization. If you can't get an article written about you, get a public service announcement. After all, you are not charging a fee to your fellow networkers, you are providing them a service. Most papers—and even some radio stations—will accept public service announcements and run them for free.

Supermarkets have bulletin boards where you can post your notice. So do some lobbies of apartment and condominium complexes. So do laundries. The moral is: Don't turn up your nose at where you post your announcement, just get it out.

Don't worry too much up front about establishing your goals and objectives. You have already identified your own personal needs and realized what you are looking for. When you meet with others, they will be eager to tell you their needs. Eventually, your organization will evolve its own goals and objectives. Those who don't seem to fit into the network will fade away, leaving the core of determined, hard working participants. At first, it is more important to get the people together. As a matter of fact, if you are too specific in saying what the network will be like and what it should accomplish, you risk alienating or turning away some who would be valuable contacts but who don't think they fit your description.

2. SET UP A TIME, DATE, AND PLACE TO MEET

While it might be counter-productive to be too specific as to the goals and format of the network, it is a good idea to be specific as to when and where the first meeting will be held. Putting a notice out saying, "People who work out of your homes, let's get together! Call 555-1212 for more information." will not get a big response. Instead, decide what date and time you want to hold the meeting. Are mornings better? Are evenings optimal? How far in advance do you want to plan the meeting? Will it happen next week? Two weeks from now? Where should the meeting be held? Is your home too personal, too informal? You may want to meet at a library, or at a YMCA or YWCA (many have rooms they rent for very small fees).

Whatever you decide, have the information down precisely. Decide also whether you want to include your own telephone number on the bulletin. If you do, you may get many pestering calls. If you don't, you might miss talking with someone who can help you but who simply can't attend the meeting.

3. BE PREPARED WITH THE PAPERWORK

Have plenty of your own business cards ready to pass out. Have brochures or other promotional literature. Most importantly for the future of your network, have a questionnaire. Ask the people for a little background about themselves, then ask them why they came to the meeting and what they want from a network. Ask also what they can contribute. (*Hint:* Ask them where they saw the notice; you'll learn where the good posting places are for the next time.) If you have access to a computer, it is a good idea to enter all of this information into a data base. You can run off copies for each participant.

4. HAVE AN AGENDA FOR THE MEETING

Before you welcome the first participant, have a clear idea what you are going to do at the meeting. An afternoon spent in haphazard conversation does not make someone want to come back and participate in a network. Start with an introduction of yourself and how you got the idea for beginning a homeworker's network. Spend less time talking about who you are (this is not the time for making a sales pitch and trying to get business) than about what the network can offer to the listeners. Then hand out the questionnaires. When they have been filled out, collect them. Discuss everyone's answers.

The discussion of the questionnaires should take up most of the first meeting, as the questionnaire (if well written) asks the questions most of the others came to the meeting to ask. When you have talked long enough, *set up the next meeting.* This is very important. Many times, meetings go well, everyone goes home happy—and that's the end of that. You've trapped your quarry; don't let 'em get away. Before you open the meeting to milling about, exchanging business cards and sad stories of being at the mercy of every door-to-door salesperson around, be certain everyone knows where and when the next meeting will be.

If feasible, set up an agenda for the next meeting. You might want to assign "homework." For example, everyone could get a second copy of the questionnaire to take home and think about more carefully. Encourage everyone to make and bring back lists of what they want from the network. Ask the others to think about establishing a regular meeting date and place or about publishing a newsletter. Decide how formal or informal you want the network to be. Remember, people who eschew the 9-to-5 world might not be amenable to a lot of regimentation.

One of the hardest aspects of working from home is the lack of feedback. At an office, you can always mosey down the hall and ask a colleague what he thought of your presentation. Therefore, in order to find out what you did well and what you can still improve, you need to make a little more effort. One technique is creating and using evaluation forms. There are two schools of thought here. One is that you should have the forms filled out at the end of the meeting, while it is still fresh in people's minds. The other is that you should mail the evaluation forms out a week or so later, when the participants have had a chance to think about the meeting. If you choose the latter course, be sure to enclose a self-addressed, stamped envelope to ensure your receiving responses.

Your evaluation form should reflect your goals. If you want to work towards a specific point, like making a network to supply numerous referrals and jobs, discuss that. However, if your network is simply to keep up with the latest news in the field, the assessment should be geared toward that. Example 7-1 is an example of an evaluation based on this latter goal.

Note: This is a basic, broad evaluation form. Use it as a guide. As you become more adept at networking, you will be able to add more personal questions or comments. The evaluation form is for *your* use and benefit; make it personal to work for you.

EVALUATION

In order to help all of us gain the most from our network, we need to find out what each member thinks of the meetings we have. Please take a moment to answer the following questions. There is space at the end for any additional comments and suggestions. A self-addressed, stamped envelope is included for your convenience.

1. TIME. Was the meeting scheduled at a convenient time for you? Would you be willing to meet at this time regularly, or do you suggest a different time?

2. LOCATION. Is the location convenient for you? Did you get adequate directions to the meeting? Do you prefer to meet regularly at the same location, or to vary meeting sites?

3. NOTIFICATION. How were you notified of the meeting? Did you have enough advance notice, or were you shuffling your plans at the last moment?

4. SIZE. Were there too many people at the meeting? Too few? What size do you feel is ideal?

5. PARTICIPANTS. Were the people at the meeting those whom you wanted to meet? Can you suggest additional people to include?

6. AGENDA. Do you prefer to know ahead of time what the agenda is, or do you want it to remain flexible? Was everything covered you felt should have been, or was there too little time?

7. LEADERSHIP. Was there too little leadership? Too much (one person monopolized the meeting)? What do you want in terms of a chairperson or leader?

GENERAL COMMENTS OR SUGGESTIONS

EXAMPLE 7-1

CONCLUSION

Networking from home can be tricky. Not everyone works in an office, where formal or informal networks abound. Those who work out of their homes have special networking needs. One key concept of this chapter was that you need to be aware of your isolation and of the negative aspects of it. These can include missing out on advance information, lack of feedback, not understanding and using the power structure, missing a chance to observe personalities and use that information, and not building up a reservoir of favors given and favors owed.

We hope you've learned more about how to remain in an existing network (if you have quit your office job, but want to remain in the network). We hope you are more aware of both the advantages and the disadvantages of working at home, in terms of remaining in an existing network or creating a new network. In this chapter, our goal was to help you learn more about yourself, what you want (determining your needs), what you have to offer (identifying your resources), what specific help you need (identifying your missing resources). We presented specific steps you can take to help yourself network effectively, whether that network is one you've been in for years or a new one of your own making. Use the evaluation and assessment forms in this chapter. You will find that with a little practice, you can learn from them and use them to maximize your potential. Working from home doesn't have to mean losing contact with the business community. You can remain as involved as ever, if you know the techniques.

8
SURMOUNTING REJECTION TO DEVELOP STRONG AND DURABLE NETWORKS

*R*ejection. Can you think of a more depressing word? When you hear the term, can't you just visualize Charlie Chaplin's Little Tramp, being turned away from a possible job or being kicked out of a bread line for already having dined that day (such a fine meal he made of his shoe!) The man walks away, rejected, the picture of defeat and unhappiness, shoulders slumped, head bowed, toes dragging in the dust.

We've all been rejected in our personal lives. Can you remember when you were sixteen and going to a party was the most important thing in the world to you? You asked someone to go with you and were rejected. Kindly, cruelly—it really didn't matter. Mother Teresa herself could have given you a gentle, "No, thanks" and you would have been just as rejected and just as crushed.

As we got older, we saw that rejection was a fact of professional life as well. We interviewed for jobs we didn't get, suggested programs that weren't adopted, recommended changes in letters that were filed and never saw the light of day again. Some rejections we halfway expected (as a colleague once said ruefully to us, "Somehow, I knew in my heart of hearts that the boss was not going to buy the idea of holding our convention in Tahiti!"). Sometimes we thought we had meritorious suggestions, but understood and accepted and respected the reasons for the rejection ("While we do need a new telephone system, I can see that the firm doesn't want to make any changes until it determines whether we are going to merge with another company and move offices."). Some rejections just plain hurt ("There's absolutely no reason my supervisor had to reject my idea of child care; we have the space, the money, and the need.")

Because networking is a part of life, it has its good and bad times, as well. Some people have networks in which there are all good times: Everyone enjoys networking, is delighted and honored to be a part of the network, is willing to give and take as necessary to make the network go. Those people should be enshrined under glass for everyone to see. Their numbers are dwindling every day. For the rest of us, networking doesn't always work. There are times when people reject the very idea of being a part of our system; other times people accept membership in the network, but reject the concomitant obligations. What happens then?

WHAT IS REJECTION?

There are many ways a networker can experience rejection. Let's examine just a few of them.

1. NO ONE WANTS TO JOIN THE PARTY

Jean has been working at Mosher Technology Enterprises for
four years. She has just graduated from business school, having gone nights for, as she puts it, "the best years of my life
. . . and the longest!" One of her classes at business school
had been taught by a professor who discussed networking at
length. Jean is enthusiastic about the concept, certain she can
make it work at MTE. She spends hours drawing up her plans,
getting the idea of her network structure, goals, and purposes
clear in her mind. She discusses the idea with several of her
co-workers and is surprised by their lukewarm, barely courteous reception. The more Jean talks about networking, trying
to make the others catch fire and be as enthusiastic as she is,
the more she finds herself being avoided in the halls. Finally,
a friend tells her point blank, "Jean, no one here is interested
in your networking idea. We are all scientists, loners. We were
hired here with the promise that we would be left alone to do
our experiments. All we want is lab time and equipment; this
isn't a social set."

Talk about rejection! Jean barely got the word "networking" out of her mouth when her co-workers made it clear
they were not interested. This is rejection at the grass roots
level: The whole concept is dismissed immediately.

2. THE OVERWORKED HOST

Kevin had a different saga than Jean. He is a salesperson for
a large office supply firm. The workers make no commissions,
just a straight salary. They do, however, all share in the profits
at the end of the year. Therefore, any increase in sales by anyone will ultimately benefit everyone. Kevin has been reading
a lot about networking lately and has decided it will work to
everyone's advantage. "After all," he reasons, "If we pool our resources, we can make more logical territorial assignments, be
more fair with the customer pool. Everyone will save time and
make more money." At the weekly meeting of the salespeople,
Kevin proposes his idea. Everyone sees the merit of it immediately, and congratulates Kevin, who leaves rather smug and

proud of himself. However, as the days go on, Kevin's smugness turns to exhaustion. Everyone is willing to join the network, but only Kevin seems to be doing any work.

Kevin is the one who collects all the back data on the customers. Kevin is the one who nags the salespeople to give him their records. Kevin is the one who collates and distributes everything. Kevin is the one who is getting pretty sick and tired of being the only one working at networking. "I thought this was a great idea, and so did everyone else," he says. "Now I see that they are all willing to share in the profits that result, but they are not willing to put in the hard work to get those profits. This is not my idea of networking, just of working."

Kevin's rejection was different from Jean's. Jean's colleagues were not interested in the idea of networking at all. Kevin's associates immediately saw the advantages of networking and embraced the concept eagerly, but made Kevin do all the work. They rejected the extra effort that networking would take.

3. WHO BROUGHT THE BEST DATE TO THE PARTY?

Sometimes, networking is rejected due to incredible competition. This often happens in offices where there are few chances for advancement or in firms where pay is based mainly on commissions.

Cathy works as a manager at a very upscale clothing store. The store is known for its personal service. When Cathy was hired, she was happy to hear that "we are all part of the family; we all help one another out." Cathy had worked in retail sales for years, and was tired of the cutthroat competition for customers. However, her new firm pays a small salary and a large commission, just as her former employers did.

Cathy, in the flush of first enthusiasm, drew up a networking plan. She met with the salesclerks to discuss sharing customer lists, helping out with regular customers when a salesclerk is ill or busy. At first, her coworkers listened and nodded. After a little while, however, Cathy sensed that the atmosphere in the room was becoming tense. "You'd have thought that I asked them to give up their own children," she later lamented. "All I wanted to do was get us working together as a team, let us help each other. They all acted as if I were taking the food out of their mouths. All I heard were 'what-if's' that revolved around who would get the commission and how the commission would be split. They just couldn't see that networking would help us all in the long run."

Cathy learned a very real lesson about rejection. It occurs much more frequently when money is involved. It is one thing to say "Let's network!" when people are salaried, quite another when there are commissions, and thus built-in competition.

What do the jeremiads of Jean, Kevin, and Cathy have in common? They are all rejected attempts to network on a large scale. That is, the three workers were attempting to create networks using their firms and all the employees. Rejection occurred in various forms, but was total. Have you ever tried to organize a company-wide (or larger) network? If so, you probably have a rejection tale of your own. Friends and co-workers could tell you their stories as well. Of course, it doesn't have to be that way. While failure is a fact of life, facts change. How could Jean, Kevin, and Cathy have come back from failure, turned around rejection to make their networks work?

TURNING LARGE-SCALE REJECTION INTO WHOLESALE ACCEPTANCE

1. JEAN

As you recall, Jean had the most dramatic rejection. No one at her firm was willing even to consider networking. The loners were proud of their solitude, not only content but desirous of being alone. The scientists considered that not having to be part of a network was one of the perks of the job. How can Jean turn their attitudes around? Should she even try?

Good question: Should Jean try to establish a network at work, or was the whole idea a bad one? There may very well be times when networking, as we know it, is *not* feasible for any number of reasons. However, note the careful phrasing: Networking *as we know it.* Just as no two people are alike, no two networks will be alike. Jean needs to reevaluate *why* she wants a network, what benefits she thinks will accrue from having one, and what is in it for her co-wokers. By doing so, she will determine as well what type of network to have. Given the nature of the people at her firm, the network will almost certainly not be the textbook type her teacher talked about in business school. It will be a looser, more informal, scientific type of network, one that the scientists can think of as more technical, less social. If Jean is shrewd, she won't call the system a "network" at all, but will choose another term more dear to the hearts of scientists. One good idea might be *synergism,* defined as "the simultaneous action of separate agencies, which, together, have greater total effect than the sum of their individual effects." Scientists are familiar and comfortable with the term. As marketers, snake oil salesmen, and Borsht Belt comedians say, "Know your audience!"

2. KEVIN

Kevin's rejection was different. His colleagues accepted the idea of networking, but rejected the necessary effort needed to make it work. Since the idea was Kevin's, they reasoned that the effort would be Kevin's as well. All they would share would be the benefits. What can Kevin do?

He might decide that since he has been informally elected Head of the Network, he should act like one. He can create lists detailing the tasks and responsibilities of each person. Instead of asking people to help, he can simply hand out orders and imply that each person will do his duty; after all, "all the others are cooperating; you wouldn't want to be the only slacker, would you?" Making these lists and delegating responsibilities would entail a lot of work up front, but would greatly reduce Kevin's workload down the line. He has to decide whether the benefits of networking are sufficient to merit this extra work.

3. CATHY

Cathy's rejection was for perhaps the most common reason. It's a competitive world out there. Everyone wants to know "what's in it for me?" and can rarely see beyond individual gain. Stores recognize that very human characteristic by giving sales commissions. Cathy's best way of dealing with the rejection of her networking idea is to make the workers see what *is* in it for them.

Cathy can draw up a list of advantages that will accrue to each person who joins and actively participates in the network. She should be very, very specific, giving (if at all possible) actual dollars and cents projections of benefits. It does little good to sound like a cheerleader and bleat, "Just think of the good feelings you will have from being part of our Happy Sales Family!" To those who are out there working hard for a few dollars, it is much more enticing to hear, "We estimate that your sales will increase $100 a week if you participate in our network. That's $5,000 a year: the cost of sending a child to college, the cost of a great vacation, almost the cost of a new car!" Hey, for a new car, wouldn't *you* be willing to work at networking?

The above three stories are common. In each instance, the individual has attempted networking on a grand scale and has failed on the same grand scale. You have read about common reasons for rejection and been given suggested solutions to that rejection. In your own day-to-day life, you probably don't deal on this large a scale. If you want to initiate a firm-wide network, you do so infrequently. More commonly, you want to make an existing network better, more effective, more useful to you personally. And there lies more possible rejection. Let's examine this smaller scale rejection, see what occurs, and how to handle and overcome it.

HAVING A REQUEST FOR NETWORKING REFUSED

Sometimes, networking is just another way of saying "please do me a favor." When you ask a friend or someone close to you for something, you label it a favor. When you make a request of a person whom you know only casually, or through a friend, you call it networking. Friend or co-worker, each could very well refuse your request. That happened to Steve.

1. STEVE

Let's call this unequivocal rejection. There is no debate on the matter; Ken is unwilling to network with Steve. The reasons certainly are valid, but understanding and even empathizing doesn't help Steve. He is still without his introduction.

2. CHERYL

Cheryl had worked three years ago with Doug. They had had a pleasant relationship, purely professional. Each respected the other's work. When Cheryl left the firm, Doug took her to lunch and asked her to stay in touch. Now, Cheryl is having her house remodeled. She recalls that Doug's wife is an architect. While Cheryl already has an architect of her own, she wants a second opinion on the cost of redoing the family room. Cheryl doesn't have a lot of money. She is hoping that instead of hiring a stranger and paying a great deal to have him just come out, gaze around, do a few calculations, and give an opinion (as Cheryl sees it), she can get away with having a friend, or a friend of a friend, give her an opinion. To be honest, Cheryl is looking for a freebee.

Cheryl calls Doug and explains the situation, asking him to ask his wife "to take just a few minutes to come glance around. Tell her I'll treat her to lunch." After hearing that comment, and knowing Cheryl as he does, Doug is certain that Cheryl intends to have Merlene (Doug's wife) do the work for free. He is too embarrassed to bring up money, feeling uncomfortable and uncertain whether this type of second opinion really is easy to give or not. He discusses the situation with Merlene, who hits the roof. "I am expected to take my time and use my professional skills to give an opinion that I might have to testify over, or be held responsible for, sometime in the future if there is a problem! I can't just go out there and eyeball the place and give an okay. I have a legal and an ethical responsibility to do a good job, which means *work* which means *pay*. You tell this woman what my fees are, or tell her no." Doug, unhappy but understanding, rejects Cheryl's request. He doesn't tell her why, just that his wife won't give a second opinion.

Cheryl senses that Doug really wants to help her, and can't understand why he won't. In her family, a request from one family member is automatically honored, at whatever the price. She considers this an inexplicable rejection.

3. SKIP

Skip wants to join a club that has a very exclusive membership list. The shakers and movers of the city are in the club; membership provides important contacts. As an attorney just starting a practice, Skip knows that he could get clients at the club. His former law school professor, Dean, is a member of the club and has spoken about it often in class. In a very polite, professional letter, Skip asks Dean to sponsor him for membership in the club. Weeks go by and there is no response from Dean. Skip sends a second letter and follows it up with a telephone call. The letter is not answered. The call puts Skip in touch with Dean, who rather curtly says, "I am no longer a member of that club myself. Good luck with your practice." This is yet a third type of rejection. Call it rejection by impossibility. It is not so much that Dean *won't* put up Skip for membership, but that he *can't* do so.

OVERCOMING INDIVIDUAL REJECTION

In the Jean, Kevin, and Cathy stories, it wasn't the specific request of the individual that was rejected but the whole idea of networking, or the effort involved in the project as a whole. In the scenarios involving Steve, Cheryl, and Skip, the people made—and had rejected—particular requests for networking. Sometimes rejection of particular requests are harder to deal with because we take them more personally. However, they too can be dealt with in a professional manner.

1. STEVE

Steve understood why his request was denied, but really wanted that interview. He came up with another idea. "I wrote Ken a letter, telling him in detail exactly what I wanted, and that I understood I was asking him a great deal. In the letter, I very specifically said that I would deem it a personal favor if he would just forward my letter to Valerie. He didn't have to write to her himself, or talk to her, just address the envelope. It worked. Ken put my letter in another envelope and mailed it off without adding anything. He never heard from Valerie, but I did. She telephoned me, and I got my interview."

2. CHERYL

Finally, it dawned on Cheryl (known for having to use a crowbar to open her wallet) that Merlene might want to be paid. Cheryl mentioned the idea to Doug, who talked it over with Merlene. Merlene gave Doug a list of her prices, discounted for "friendship." Cheryl compared the discounted price to other undiscounted ones, and accepted the deal. After an initial rejection, the network worked.

3. SKIP

There wasn't a lot Skip could do about Dean's rejection. If Dean is no longer a member of the club, and only club members can sponsor prospective members, Dean can't do Skip the favor Skip wants. However, Skip realized that Dean probably still has friends in the club. A second call elicited the names and telephone numbers of two of Dean's friends. Skip took them to lunch and found himself not one, but two sponsors. The persistence resulted in a happy ending, thanks to networking skills.

REJECTION: A CALL TO ACTION

You have seen how many ways networking can be rejected, on both a large and a small scale. In the scenarios, you've seen how good networking skills can overcome the rejection and get the desired outcome. Let's be more specific now, and go through steps one by one that you can use.

WHEN YOU RECEIVE A REJECTION . . .

1. EVALUATE YOUR REQUEST'S TONE

Ever hear yourself on a tape recorder? Like most of us, you probably said, "Whaaa? That can't be me. I don't sound like that at all." We never think we sound the way we do. When you made your request, how did you sound? The following are just a few of the most common tone or attitude problems many people have when making a request that is immediately rejected.

A. DEMANDING. Is anything more irritating than asking a favor and sounding as if having that favor done is your God-given right? Even if the words are polite ("Would you please give me an introduction to your supplier?"), the tone might be intimidating. We have heard people make harsh requests ("Would you *please* introduce me to your supplier?") that sound like threats. If you make it sound as if a rejection of your request will bring down the wrath of The Enforcer on the listener's head, you may just irritate him or her sufficiently to have your request rejected out of hand.

B. WHINING. If you have children, you know how whining can get on your nerves. Elongated consonants rank right up there with nails on a chalkboard for irritation: "Pllllllllllllease?" is guaranteed to send anyone out of the room.

C. BEGGING. You are not asking for the donation of a kidney. Don't make your request sound as if the person is going to do you a favor that will result in your naming your firstborn child after her. Sometimes, when we are begged to do something, perversity takes over and we refuse just because we have so much power. It's not a kind trait, but it is a very human one.

D. LACKADAISICAL. This is the opposite of begging. If you toss off the request too casually, making it seem as if it is no big deal, the listener is not going to feel the least bit hesitant in rejecting your request. In fact, he might do so automatically, on the principle that if he rejects all the minor requests, he can be a Big Man when he finally accedes to your major request.

2. EVALUATE THE TIMING AND LOCALE OF YOUR REQUEST

Maybe you asked for something in a nice, courteous tone, but did so at the wrong time in the wrong place. If your listener just got chewed out by the boss or has to go to the dentist in a few hours, his frame of mind is not going to be conducive to helping anyone but himself. If you ask in the right tone and at the right time, but in his office, rather than yours, you might not have as good a chance for acceptance. There is something to Territory Power. Make the request in your own office, on your own turf, where you are in control. Be sensitive to someone else's needs.

3. EVALUATE THE REASONABLENESS OF YOUR REQUEST

Just what are you asking the person to do? As Steve found, asking Ken to introduce him personally to Valerie was too much. It was cruel, inhumane, unreasonable. However, asking Ken just to forward a letter was reasonable. If you ask a salesperson for his client list, you probably are unreasonable. If you, however, ask him for tips on how to get one of your own, flatter him that you seek his knowledge, not his hard-won clients, you may get even more than you asked for. Think about the results, the long term effect on the person who can honor your request. If doing you a favor could cost him time, money, or the respect of others (that is, he makes you look good at his own expense), you are going to be rejected.

All right, you have reevaluated your request. You made it in a polite, courteous tone at the right time and place. The request was reasonable. Yet, it was still rejected. What now?

1. IDENTIFY AND TRY ALTERNATE SOURCES

If someone rejects your request, you could (a) give up, (b) ask him again, (c) go to someone else, or (d) reevaluate your goals. We'll go into each of these; for now, let's consider alternate sources. Is this person the only one in your office or in your circle of friends who can honor your request? Maybe you went to her simply because she was closest, or because you thought you had the best chance of success with her. Make a list of others who could help you and try them. In most instances, it is better to try someone else before going back to a person who has already denied your request. Exhaust all channels. You have to take the right steps, go through the ranks. Then, if everyone else rejects you, you have a strong case for going back to the first person and asking again.

2. DECIDE WHETHER THE REQUEST IS WORTH FIGHTING FOR

Like children at Christmas, we all ask for a lot of things we don't expect to get and might not know what to do with if we got them. Attorneys customarily ask for huge sums in court cases, but would be delighted with a fraction of that amount. When we ask for raises, we go in with inflated requests, giving ourselves something to bargain with. The same is true in networking. If you make a request that is rejected, is it worth your time and effort to try to overcome that rejection? Do you really need that introduction, that list, that whatever? If not, or if you don't need it right now, forget it. Save your requests for things you really need. If not, soon you will be like the boy who cried, "Wolf," someone to whom no one ever listens.

3. LIST THE ADVANTAGES THAT WILL ACCRUE TO EVERYONE

As mentioned earlier, we all want to know what we are going to get out of doing something. When you did the previous step, deciding whether the request was worth fighting for, the rejection worth appealing, you thought about what *you* would get out of the granted request. Now, decide what the person who will be granting the request will get out of it. The following are just a few of the many advantages that can convince people to change their minds.

- financial gain (a bonus, a raise, profit sharing)
- financial savings (getting a tax deduction, getting something for free or at a lower cost)
- increased job security
- increased respect of others (this is a good catch-all category; everyone likes to feel looked-up to)

- attention/recognition (the old "the boss will notice you" ploy)
- increased network visibility

You can probably think of dozens more possible advantages. As a matter of fact, it is a good idea to keep track of the benefits that others promise *you* so that you can use them as bait yourself in the future. When you find yourself changing your mind about a rejection, determine what it was that made you do the about-face. Bettie keeps a card file called "Inducements." It is very useful when she has to get a favor done quickly, and wants to present her case in the most favorable light. Her catalog was created with self-inducements, but has been expanded to include her ideas of what will entice colleagues. For example, she knows that money will capture Alan's attention every time, while the whiff of prestige makes Keith putty in her hands.

4. PRACTICE YOUR PRESENTATION

Vary the second request. If you made a verbal request the first time and were rejected, put your second request in writing. If your first request was very formally presented on letterhead stationery, ask a second time verbally in an informal environment, like at lunch. After all, you already know what didn't work; why do the same thing a second time?

Don't be afraid to practice. You practice your presentations to clients, don't you? You practice before an interview, making your long-suffering spouse or friends listen to you practice hundreds of variations on, "I want the job for the *challenge* it presents to me." If you're married, you probably practiced proposing or accepting a proposal hundreds of time before The Big Day. In short, practicing makes you feel more confident and comfortable. You know that the odds are against you because you have already been rejected. You can use all the help you can get.

ACCEPTING A FINAL REJECTION

Sometimes, nothing works. You want to create a network or use it, and others don't. You tried your best, made a logical, well-presented appeal of the rejection, and failed again. You really want to have your request granted, but you must accept the fact that it won't be. What now?

1. DON'T NAG

If you continue to harp on a topic, soon people will begin tuning you out, certain they know what you are going to say before you open your mouth. If you continue to plead your case when it is obviously lost, you alienate those around you. You lose their respect as well. You may think you are ennobling yourself in their eyes by being a "never-say-die" kind of person. On the contrary. Many of your associates will brand you a fool for not knowing when you've lost, for wasting your time and theirs.

2. DON'T BROOD

What good is it going to do to play martyr, to think all the time about "what could have been" if only people had networked with you? That way lies madness. Take the time to analyze what went wrong and why. Probably, in most of the cases, the fault was not yours. Don't punish yourself for something you don't control.

3. ACCEPT REJECTION GRACEFULLY

This is the hardest part of rejection for many people. Didn't you just absolutely hate it when your mother said to you, as you were suffering from the teenager's malady of a broken

heart, "Well, at least you learned something from the experience." Ann can remember giving her father a look that would
blister paint when he told her to go shake her opponent's hand
after she lost a tennis match. She did so, playing the good sport
game, but every fiber of her being rebelled. The same is true
after any defeat, any loss. When you lose the chance to network, accept defeat like a professional. Let the other person
know that you appreciate her hearing you out at least. If you
understand the other person's reasons for rejecting your request, say so.

Karen had a friend in New York who sometimes went
to Washington, D.C. Karen asked her friend, Marcy, to make a
special trip to go to D.C. in the next month to get information
on the intern program. Marcy refused, saying that she was in
the middle of finals and couldn't take the time. Now, that's a
valid reason. Karen recognized that she was asking a favor,
something the person, even though she was a friend, didn't
have to do. Therefore, her response was like this.

"Just writing to say 'Thanks anyway' regarding your
going to D.C. for me. I certainly understand that you don't have
the time right now. I remember finals all too well; it was hard
to find time for luxuries like eating and sleeping, let alone
traveling! Good luck on your exams!"

Karen managed the rejection in a positive, professional
way. She empathized with the person (we all want to feel that
someone understands) and let her off the hook. She didn't try
to make her friend feel guilty. Karen didn't go on and on about
her own problems, but gave a quick thank you and signed off.
She has left Marcy feeling relieved that Karen is not angry or
annoyed, happy that she wasn't made to feel guilty.

CONCLUSION

Rejection comes with all sorts of aftershocks. Sometimes, rejection is absolutely devastating, crushing our hopes to do or
create something wonderful. Sometimes, it is mild, a mere an-

noyance we can work around. Almost always, it is personally distressing, making us feel insecure, uncertain of our skills and (let's be honest) our popularity.

It's important to recognize that in establishing, maintaining, and working within networks, there will be rejection. For good reasons and bad, people will not do what you ask them to do. You can increase your satisfaction with your professional life by understanding rejection and dealing with it in a professional manner, overcoming it when possible and accepting it gracefully when necessary.

9
NETWORKING FOR SALES AND CUSTOMER SERVICE SUCCESS

*H*ave you seen the cartoon drawings of winged money? In the funny papers, someone pulls out a dollar bill and sees it sprout wings and take off, never to be seen again. As consumers, you and I are familiar with the concept of supersonic spending. We earn the money slowly and painstakingly, yet spend it at an alarmingly swift rate. In some situations, the money, once departed, is never seen or heard from again. The clerk takes the cash, gives you a hard and insincere smile, and turns to the next customer. That cash, for which you worked so strenuously, has ceased to work for you because the clerk and the business have ceased to work for you.

But let's imagine another situation. You still have to part with your money, but now it seems to have an aftereffect. The clerk takes the money, gives you a sincere smile, and asks you to fill out a form with your name and address so that she can put you on her mailing list. A few weeks later, you get a circular telling you in advance of a sale at the store. Your money went one step further than just making the original purchase; it gave you an early entry to a future sale, met a second set of needs for you.

Which store would you patronize a second time, one which took your money and ran, or one which took your money and built a relationship with you? Like most of us, you would go back to the store that seemed to care about you, the business that took the time to identify and attempt to meet your needs. You would go to the store that provided customer service.

THE FUNCTION OF BUSINESS

"The purpose of a business is to create and keep a customer. To do that, you want to do those things that will make people want to do business with you."

PROFESSOR LEAVITT
Harvard University
Marketing Imagination.

Whether you are in a service or sales business, you need customers. You have to sell your service or product to someone. While it might be romantic to think of yourself as a starving painter, creating masterpieces in an unheated garrett, it is more satisfying to picture yourself selling your works and spending the money on a good meal and a good time. As businesspeople, we need to develop *and maintain* a good customer base. That maintenance is where networking comes in.

For sales and customer service, networking serves two functions. By networking with others, you find your customers in the first place. Referrals and suggestions can help you become known, make your product familiar to those who need it. By networking with your own customers, you ensure their continued loyalty. This customer loyalty can make the difference between your firm becoming a statistic, one of those many businesses that fail each year, or an institution that will celebrate its centennial. Since networking with customers is so important, let's examine it in more detail.

HOW TO CREATE AN ON-GOING NETWORKING RELATIONSHIP WITH YOUR CUSTOMERS

Personalities do affect how much businesspeople do together. No matter how professional you are, you naturally prefer to do business with someone with whom you have a good rapport than with a cold, unfeeling person, highly skilled though he or she may be. Remember the old saying, "You catch more flies with honey than with vinegar"? Old sayings get to be old and clichéd by overuse for a very good reason: They have a lot of truth in them. If you are or have ever been in sales, you know that half the battle is won if your customer just plain likes you. How can you build a good rapport with your customers?

1. BLEND YOUR COMMUNICATION STYLE WITH THAT OF YOUR CUSTOMERS

No one is asking a leopard to change his spots, here. If you are a hail-fellow-well-met, blustering type of person, you are not going to be able to pull off the act of a cosmopolitan, urbane person. You would look foolish trying to be something that you are not, and would probably alienate, rather than ingratiate, yourself. However, that does not mean you can't attempt to reach a common communications ground. What *style* of communication does your customer favor?

Is your customer the type who really enjoys chatting about family, the ball game, the weather, and a myriad of other topics before getting down to business? Some people find it difficult to jump right in and start taking purchase orders. There are those who find it rude to do so, not just unpleasant. Others pride themselves on their own homey style of business and think they are making the whole business atmosphere more relaxed and pleasant by talking about outside topics for a while. We can remember one customer who felt he was an excellent judge of human nature and thought that anyone who wasn't willing to shoot the breeze before getting down to business was hiding something and was not the type of person with whom to do business. He was obviously someone who could be sold with a technique called **relationship selling.** We highly recommend an interesting and amusing (and useful) book on this subject, *Relationship Selling* by Jim Cathcart (see the Suggested Readings in the Appendix). Jim would agree with this customer. In fact, the theme of Jim's book is that a sale *never* takes place until a relationship is established.

Is your customer the opposite type, one who is no-nonsense, all business? She may be impatient of inquiries about her family and want to keep just to the business at hand. A hurried or harassed person will resent you for taking her time for pleasantries.

What kind of a sense of humor does your customer have? If she has an excellent one, practice a few jokes and hit her with them. If she doesn't like long jokes but adores puns, the more noisome the better, save up several for the next time you see her. If the customer doesn't like jokes or doesn't get yours, take the hint and end your show business career as far as she is concerned.

The moral is to *identify* the communication style of your customer and, as far as possible, *match* it. Doing so, will make you more comfortable around the customer and make him more relaxed around you. You will build a rapport that encourages a long-term relationship.

2. YOU MUST KNOW AND APPRECIATE THE CUSTOMER'S NEEDS

You are not in sales or customer service to judge the cus-tomers. It is irrelevant what your personal opinion of the customer's needs is. For example, you might think it absolutely ridiculous that a large firm has poor internal communication. Ridiculous or not, the customer has a need for duplicate memos and several copies of letters to go to different departments. Rather than assuming that your service will be shared among the various divisions, you communicate directly with those divisions, taking the time and effort to send extra letters and memos.

What if you are not certain what your customer needs? Each person and firm has slightly different requirements. The best way to identify customer needs is to ask. Everyone loves to talk, especially about his own problems and wants. Ask your customer what he wants, what he needs, what you can do for him. If he feels that you are asking because you sincerely want to know, not just because your mother taught you that it's good manners to ask what you can do for someone, he will be only too glad to bend your ear. A significant part of networking involves listening. Listen, listen, listen—and learn.

3. SHOW YOUR CUSTOMERS YOU CARE

Some people go overboard separating personal and professional lives. You may not want to socialize with your customers for many reasons, ranging from a sincere belief that business and personal activities don't mix to not having enough time to spend with your own family, let alone with Joe Blow from the company you call on twice a week (you may already see more of him than you would like). However, that does not mean you should treat your customers any worse than you treat your personal friends. When you have a friend, you do nice things for him. You may see a card he would get a kick out of and mail it to him. You might pick up a doughnut for him on your way to work. In dozens of little ways, you show your friend you care. That's what friendship is all about.

Showing you care is what networking is all about as well. No one is suggesting that you spend your inheritance on gifts for all your customers. However, there is nothing wrong with giving, either physically or emotionally. You can give something as small and free as a cartoon or an article you clipped out of the paper, thinking your customer would enjoy it. We know we feel good when those who sell to us send us cartoons with the note, "This made me think of you" or "I thought you'd appreciate this." We feel the person cares enough to make that little extra effort, has us in mind, *thinks of us as people, not just as a sale.* You can also show you care by giving a little of yourself. Call just to say hello. Wish a person well on a new project. Pass along a compliment you heard.

Too often, we are wrapped up in keeping a professional image to the detriment of common humanity. If you want to keep a customer, show him that you value him.

4. BUILD A TRUST BETWEEN YOU AND YOUR CUSTOMER

Ultimately, it all comes down to trust. Have you ever seen a little child trying to learn to ride a two-wheel bicycle? Her father will be running alongside, holding the bike, as the child is screaming, "Daddy, don't let go! Hold on, Daddy, hold on!" It is only the child's trust in her father that keeps her going.

Sometimes, it is a customer's trust in you that enables her to keep going, to take a risk she otherwise would not attempt. A customer, knowing that you can deliver by the date you say, might place an extra large order. A customer who trusts your word that you will not pass along information might tell you something that can be valuable to you professionally or personally. A customer who trusts that you are treating her honestly will recommend you to her boss or to a new firm if she transfers companies.

How can you build trust? It begins with honesty. Know what you can and cannot do, and be open about both. If your firm simply cannot guarantee a certain delivery date, state that while you will make every effort, you don't want the customer to consider the date 100-percent certain. By hedging your bets, you don't look (as some people believe) uncertain and wishy-washy. Instead, you look honest, reliable, and professional. There is no shame in not being able to do something, only in promising to do what cannot be done. If you let the customer down once, her trust in you is damaged.

5. ALWAYS TRY YOUR BEST

Is there anything worse than knowing that a project you cherished and worked hard on failed because someone else didn't try her best? A customer of yours might be knocking herself out trying to make something work, only to have you sabotage the project because of a lackadaisical attitude. Even if the project succeeds, your customer might be resentful of how lightly you treated it. You can't really tell how important a project is to a person. A customer might ask you for something in a very casual, matter of fact way, implying that it is of minor importance. Yet, when you treat it that way, you are dismayed to find that your cavalier tactics have cost you a customer. You showed that you didn't care, that you weren't taking the customer seriously. Do your best every time.

6. BE THERE

Perhaps the most important facet of creating an on-going networking relationship with your customers is your physical presence. Be there for your customers. How can you expect to establish and maintain a good relationship if you are always gone? Let the customer know when and where to contact you, how to get ahold of you personally. I know of one super-saleswoman who handed out SASE to her customers, complete with the stamped message, "Top priority." Everyone who got a set of those envelopes was assured that anything sent in one would receive immediate attention. How do you think those customers felt? They considered themselves pretty special and were confident that they could get their message directly to the salesperson. Other people give their customers direct line numbers. The proliferation of 800 (toll-free) numbers in recent years has shown that big businesses are becoming more and more aware of the need to be available to their customers.

     The personal touch is critical. Form letters, while a fact of life, depress most of us. A personal letter, a telephone call, or a personal visit are the keys to keeping customers. Show with your physical presence that you value the customer and are interested in her business.

MATCH NETWORKING WITH YOUR SALES GOALS

Networking works for you, as well as for your customers. You are in this together. In order to gain the maximum advantage yourself from networking, you need to understand your own goals. Once you have identified these, you can see how networking can help you achieve them.

1. WHY ARE YOU IN SALES?

What were your reasons for entering a sales career? Do you enjoy working with people? Are you good with the product, and consider selling a necessary evil? Did you fall into sales from another job? Identify your reasons for being in sales, as specifically as possible.

2. WHAT ARE YOUR SALES GOALS?

Where do you see yourself at the end of this year? In five years? In ten years? When do you want to retire, and how? Your goals help shape how you network. For example, if you are in sales now but want to get into management, you will want to network with those who are in administrative positions, as well as with your normal customers. On the other hand, if you love sales and intend to be a seller for the rest of your career, you want to concentrate on networking with the buyers, not the managers. Do you want to make one or two big sales a year, or have a steady stream of purchases all year long? Do you want to concentrate on one or two big customers, or sell to many different smaller firms? Your sales goals all contribute to your overall networking plan.

3. WITH WHICH CUSTOMERS DO YOU WORK BEST?

Realistically, you are going to enjoy working with some of your customers, and barely tolerate being with others. It is important that you identify your strong and weak bases. Depending on your goals, you might need to work harder at your weak bases, networking to get more business from the customers with whom you have traditionally not done too well. Or, you may decide that you can eliminate those customers and use your network to gain new ones.

    Bonus: Your network can open your eyes to a different answer to this question. You might consider that you do a fine job with Firm X, that it is one of your success stories. Through your network, you could have the disheartening (but salutary) experience of learning that Firm X is dissatisfied with your performance and is considering going with another seller. It is easy to sink into a routine with a customer, to think that since you "have him locked up," you can slack off a bit. Networking keeps you on your toes.

4. HOW DOES YOUR NETWORK SUPPORT YOU AND YOUR GOALS?

Once you have identified your goals and thought some about your strengths and weaknesses, it is time to match your new-found knowledge with your understanding of your network. A network is a tool, something you use to help yourself and others. Be certain that it is the most effective tool it can be. You wouldn't use a hammer to pound in a spark plug; you'd use a wrench to tighten it. You shouldn't use a network that is geared one way for a customer base that is geared a different way.

    Spend some time thinking about the match between your network and your goals. If you really want to concentrate on one specific product, rather than on a whole line, your network should consist of people who are specialists in the market for that product. Working with generalists, small mom and pop firms that have a need for just a little bit of everything, is not the best use of your networking skills. If your goal is to move from sales to management, to open your own firm, you will want to expand your network beyond people in positions analogous to your own. You'll want to get together with those people who have different skills than yours, people who can do, or can recommend others to do, the bookkeeping, advertising, computer work.

WORK SMARTER, NOT HARDER

Are you thinking right about now that this networking stuff seems almost more trouble than it is worth? While the reaction is not uncommon, it is not correct. Networking can be a lot of trouble, but it is worth every moment of effort. Networking's purpose is to facilitate matters, to make your life and your tasks easier. In customer service, if you have a good networking relationship with your customers, you have a more pleasant working environment, a greater opportunity for making sales, and a brighter future. Networking can make you work smarter, not harder. Unfortunately, there are some traps that a person can fall into while networking—traps that do make you work too hard. Let's review some of these now, so that you can recognize and avoid them later.

1. COOPERATION vs. COMPETITION

A little competition is good. It is inescapable in sales, since every buyer has dozens of would-be sellers clamoring for her attention. However, as a networker, you want to be certain that you are competing with the right person: yourself. *You* set your goals; *you* work towards them. No one else is going to see those goals; no one else is going to keep track of your progress. Just as athletes sometimes compete against their own last performance, you compete against your own last best accomplishment.

Don't compete with the customers in your network. We have seen people become so involved in the mechanics of networking that they turn it into a full-time job instead of a tool. The network serves you, not vice versa. Work together with your customers to provide the best service you can.

2. GIVE WITHOUT EXPECTATION

Don't you just loathe those people who say, "Here's your present; now where's mine?" Of course, life is a series of quid pro quo situations. Especially in networking, what you give eventually comes back to you. However, don't give with the *expectation* that doing so will reap an immediate reward. You are giving because you sincerely want to do the best possible job you can for your customers. Going a little out of your way to help a customer is great if you do so because you want to do your best. Going out of your way because then the customer will feel obligated to you and you can hit her up for a bigger order the next time will eventually come back to haunt you. People have excellent antennae when it comes to sensing the purpose of favors. If you give only because you expect to take in the immediate future, your customers will sense the fact and resent you for it. Every customer wants to feel special, feel valued. He wants to think that you are doing something extra because it is for him and because you *want* to help *him.* When he thinks that you are just doing your duty and keeping count of the favor tally, he will resent you and your actions and may become suspicious of everything you do from than on, wondering about your ulterior motive. You end up in a worse position than if you had not done the extra work in the first place.

3. PHRASE REQUESTS FOR REFERRALS CAREFULLY

No one wants to be used. If you develop a great relationship with a customer, he probably will be only too glad to refer you to others. However, if you demand as your due the names of other firms, he may refuse to give them to you out of sheer orneriness. Your customer is aware of the fact that you want to get new business from him. Your success or failure in the endeavor depends on your approach. Think of the last time you were in a store. If the salesclerk snapped, "Whadda want?" rather than "How may I help you?" you'd be tempted to take your business elsewhere. The first question put the onus on you, made it sound as if you were disrupting the salesclerk's routine, causing problems by your importunings. The second request put the burden on the clerk. The speaker made it sound as if you were doing her a favor by letting her help her.

You can use the same tactful approach in asking for referrals. A simple, "Do you know anyone else whom I may serve, anyone else who could benefit from my products?" is good. It makes it sound as if you are going to do your best to bestow a benefit on the person whom your customer refers to you. Your customer is eager to give you the name of her friend or associates, eager to have the person helped.

Note: Be careful not to be condescending. If you place yourself above your customer, giving the impression that you think you are doing her a big favor and she's mighty lucky to have you, you can destroy a good relationship. Saying, "Now that I've solved your problem, can you tell me who else you know who needs help?" makes the customer feel terrible. Who likes feeling inferior, in need of help, even when he is? Practice several approaches. One we have always found useful is "I'm so glad we worked together to solve that problem. Now you have me flushed with our success and I'm raring to go again. Can you recommend anyone else who might be able to use my services? They can get me while I'm hot!" This comment uses humor and flattery (suggesting that the customer had a hand in the success of the project) in making the request. It's a hard one to turn down.

4. DON'T RESPOND CHURLISHLY TO FAILURE

If you are given a lead that does not pan out, be gracious. It is very easy to be disappointed and abrupt and rude when a much-hoped for, hard-won referral turns out not to be worth the struggle it took to get. For example, you may spend months cultivating a customer to get an introduction to someone in her network. When you finally get the introduction, nothing happens. For whatever reason, the new person is not interested in working with you, in becoming part of your network. Of course, you are disappointed. However, that is no reason to be rude. Respond with understanding and graciousness. Remember that just because someone does not want to do business with you at this time does not mean he will never do business with you at all.

5. DON'T BE EGOCENTRIC

To be egocentric is to think that you are the center of everything. When you network well, you can fall into the trap of thinking that you are the sun and everything else revolves around you. A skilled networker does not see himself at the center doing a good job and let it go to his head. We prefer to think of networking as a fishing net. Sure, the center has to be strong, but the rest of the net had better be in good working order as well, or the big fish will get right through. Keep it in mind that you are also a part of other people's networks, that they have large card catalogues and referral banks just as you do. What is very important—momentous to you—might be just another introduction or just another piece of business to someone else.

6. DON'T FORGET THE FOLLOW-UP

No matter *what* the outcome, no matter how unhappy or disappointed or even disgusted you are with the effect of networking, send a thank you note. If you met with someone who rejected your overtures, send a note thanking him for his time. If a prospective customer spent a lot of your time before deciding not to place an order, send him a thank you note for considering your product so carefully. If one customer mentioned your services to another firm which called for information, send the first customer a thank you note.

7. DON'T LOSE VISIBILITY

You can become so involved in paperwork and in servicing those customers you have that you shut yourself off from the community as a whole. A key to successful networking is visibility. If the customers don't know you're there, they can't come to you. Continue to attend professional conferences for exposure. Attend as many meetings as possible. Even if you don't contribute much, your presence will be noted. Others will hear that you were at the meeting and attribute to you a level of knowledge you may or may not have, and a level of caring you definitely displayed by taking the time and effort to attend. Publicize yourself through professional newsletters. Keep your business cards floating.

8. DON'T GIVE UP

Analogous to remaining visible is remaining determined. You're only human to become depressed at times, thinking that you are trying so hard and getting so little. Anyone who deals with the public knows that people can be thoughtless and cruel. Everyone has bad days. You can plan for them, just as a manufacturer plans for waste and scrap at the factory. If you have defined your goals and made a good match between networking and achieving those goals, you should keep on plugging away. Decide to be a winner, and be persistent.

9. DON'T TAKE IT ALL TOO SERIOUSLY

Relax. Have fun. Enjoy yourself. Business is business, but there's no reason you have to be somber and gloomy all the time. If you cultivate a positive, enthusiastic attitude, you will make others want to be around you. You probably have seen the bumper sticker: "Smile . . . it makes others wonder what you're up to." It's true! If you can remain upbeat and enthusiastic, showing that you are looking forward to working with your customers, you will make them want to work with you. Networking is a skill, a *part* of your life, not life itself. If you make a mistake, forgive yourself. If you lose a valued customer and see little chance of regaining her, learn from your mistake. You'll still have a reason to smile tomorrow. You want to do the best you can for your customers, to make them happy. Should you do less for yourself?

CONCLUSION

Customer service is going to become ever more important to firms in the future. It used to be that a firm "bought local," gave its business to the nearby company almost automatically. But now our world seems to be shrinking. We are all connected by trains, planes, television, computers, and satellite transmissions. We have businesses purchasing from, and selling to, third world nations. Large firms have branches scattered nationally and internationally, and they can buy wherever they want. Mere geography is not the determining factor in a purchase decision anymore. What is? Along with such obvious factors as price and quality, customer service plays an important role.

Companies are made up of people, individuals with feelings. These people want to be heard, to feel liked, to consider themselves respected. They want to know that they are valued. They need, personally and professionally, to have a good working relationship with a person whom they can trust. A good networker picks up on those feelings and provides the service the customer wants. He or she is able to parlay that customer satisfaction into new customers, new leads, and new business opportunities.

In summary, a networker:

- recognizes the importance of customer service,
- identifies his customers' needs,
- does everything he or she can to match the two sets of needs and goals and to fulfill both, and
- succeeds!

APPENDIX

WHAT IS NETWORKING?

1. Networking is giving without expectation.
2. Networking is the ability to express appreciation by saying thank you.
3. Networking is career and personal clarity.
4. Networking is an on-going relationship building process.
5. Networking is determination.
6. Networking is being willing to set realistic, achievable goals.
7. Networking is being committed to do whatever it takes to achieve your goals.
8. Networking is caring enough to do and be your very best.
9. Networking is loving yourself enough to love and give to others.
10. Networking is the ability to make all your dreams come true.
11. Networking is connecting with others to help you get the job done in the most efficient and effective manner possible.

SUGGESTED READINGS

CATHCART, JIM, *Relationship Selling.* HDL Publishing, 1987.

DEVILLE, JARD, *Nice Guys Finish First.* Morrow: New York, 1979.

EDWARDS, PAUL and SARAH, *Working From Home.* Tarcher Houghton Mifflin: Boston, 1985.

JEFFERS, SUSAN, *Feel the Fear and Do It Anyway.* Harcourt, Brace & Jovanovich: Orlando, Florida, 1987.

JOSEFOWITZ, NATASHA, *Paths to Power.* Addison-Wesley: Reading, Massachusetts, 1980.

KUCHNER, HAROLD, *When All You've Ever Wanted Isn't Enough.* Pocket Books: New York, 1965.

NAISBITT, JOHN, *Megatrends.* Warner: New York, 1984.

PEALE, NORMAN VINCENT and BLANCHARD, KEN, *The Power of Ethical Management.* William Morrow: New York, 1988.

STERN, BARBARA, *Is Networking for You?* Prentice Hall: New Jersey, 1981.

WELCH, MARY SCOTT, *Networking.* Harcourt, Brace & Jovanovich: New York, 1980.

INDEX